Being Alone

David Tuffley

I never found a companion that was so companionable as solitude.
-- Henry David Thoreau

To my beloved Nation of Four
Concordia Domi – Foris Pax

Language... has created the word 'loneliness' to express the pain of being alone. And it has created the word 'solitude' to express the glory of being alone. Paul Tillich

Published 2013, 2019 by Altiora Publications
ISBN-13: 978-1493619641 ISBN-10: 1493619640

ALTIORA
· PUBLICATIONS ·

Dr. David Tuffley is a Senior Lecturer in Applied Ethics at Griffith University in Australia. With over 60 titles in print and millions of verified downloads, David is a non-fiction author of international renown.

Beyond the English-speaking world, his work has been translated into Chinese, German and Japanese.

Become friends with David Tuffley on Facebook: facebook.com/Tuffley

Contents

Contents

Contents

Introduction

> *"Alone, alone, all, all alone,*
> *Alone on a wide wide sea!*
> *And never a saint took pity on*
> *My soul in agony."*

This quote from Coleridge's *The Rime of the Ancient Mariner* sums up the abject despair of loneliness in the extreme. An unavoidable part of the human condition, we have all experienced it to some degree.

But how do we understand loneliness? What can be done about it?

For a social creature like humans, the underlying cause of loneliness is feeling disconnected from something larger than us which sustains us at the emotional level just as food sustains us at the physical. That emotional sustenance can come from family and friends or from doing something meaningful with your time.

That is the ambitious scope of this book; exploring how to go about finding purpose and meaning in life. This is to fix the root cause of loneliness, and that is a better, more permanent solution than just treating the symptoms.

In the society of the 21st Century, an alarming statistic is apparent; the number of people reporting they are lonely is on the rise. It is leading some observers to call it an epidemic. Despite communication technology making it easier than ever to connect with people around the world, never have so many people been so lonely.

If being lonely is an unavoidable fact of life; *Being Alone* can help you or someone you know to transform the negative experience of loneliness to a positive one. And if you already enjoy solitude, *Being Alone* looks at how to enjoy the deeper dimensions of solitude.

We take a holistic approach that goes beyond the standard advice of *"you need to get out more, make new friends, meet new people, join community groups"*. This ground has been well covered already. Instead, we help you to understand the underlying nature of loneliness and what you can do about it in a positive way today.

One: The Basics

"When the snows fall and the white winds blow,
the lone wolf dies but the pack survives."
— George R.R. Martin, A Game of Thrones

There is a tension within us all, going way back to the evolutionary past that wants time by ourselves in our own headspace, and the company of other people so that we might survive in a dangerous world. We need both conditions at different times, and where each of us sits on that continuum with solitary at one end and social at the other will be different for each individual.

Sometimes the push and pull from each end of the continuum balances out. And sometimes we want what we don't have more than what we do and desire to be alone when in company, and vice versa.

It is a constantly moving target, so does it not make sense to develop the ability to remedy our own loneliness? The remedy is not complicated, it is quite easy to understand; it is the putting into practice that takes time, effort and patience.

Loneliness & Solitude

Loneliness and solitude – two words separated by a chasm of psychological space. In solitude you intuitively experience aspects of your inner life that are revealing, sometimes enlightening. You get the feeling that you have grown as a person because you better understand yourself.

Loneliness looks outside of the self and focusses on what is missing. It is like being hungry and craving food. There is a perceived lack of something, usually the company of someone special or something meaningful to do. The remedy is for that someone to come into your life or a quest to present itself. But one cannot conjure such things on demand, so for as long as the remedy is seen to be dependent on external factors over which you have little control, the feelings of loneliness will persist and perhaps deepen.

It is therefore necessary to gain control over your thinking. This can be achieved by fully accepting the fundamental truth that what happens in your own head is the only thing that you actually have control over. What happens out in the world, the way people think and act, is not controllable, although we can exert limited influence.

Anger and frustration inevitably come from expecting to control that which cannot be controlled. The wise move is to lower one's expectations about what people *should* be like, what they *should* do, how the world *should* be. By this simple act of lowering expectations means you will seldom be disappointed and often delighted when people act in ways that exceed your expectations. A recipe for a good life.

Adopt the habit of asking yourself often *"is this something I have control over?"*. If the answer is no, discipline yourself to simply not think worry about it. That's not to say ignore it, as it might be something that you need to be aware of. But to not invest mental energy in trying to control what is fundamentally uncontrollable.

The key point is that you *can* control what you think about, including what you think about being alone. That is certainly under your control.

Cultivating this independent, clear seeing, clear-thinking mind-set paves the way for creating the mind-set of someone who rarely feels lonely. As Shakespeare's Hamlet wisely observed; *there is nothing either good or bad but thinking makes it so.*

Introverts & Extraverts

The terms *introversion* and *extraversion* came in common usage in the 20th Century to distinguish a basic personality trait. Extraverts tend to be outgoing, drawing energy from their interaction with people. Introverts are inward-looking, reserved, preferring solitude to company much of the time. They get their energy from within. Too much contact with people over-stimulates them and can lead to emotional exhaustion and withdrawal.

Looking around in the world, it would seem there is a continuum of introversion-extraversion that follows a bell-curve distribution. No two people will be located in exactly the same place on the continuum, although it will be quite crowded around the middle of the curve. This is the middle ground where the competing needs for solitude and social contact can be brought into a workable compromise. Even if you feel yourself to be an extreme introvert, there are benefits to acquiring the social skills to operate around the middle. You do not need to dwell in that middle space all of the time, only when needed. This is the so-called "ambivert"; an introvert who knows how to be an extravert when the situation requires it.

Loneliness & Depression

There is a well-documented link in the psychological literature between *chronic* loneliness and depression. If you do not have the coping skills to handle being alone, you are more likely to become depressed.

Depression manifests as an engulfing apathy that sucks the enjoyment out of life and saps your motivation to do things. You lose the motivation to do the things you used to enjoy doing. As the condition progresses, it becomes difficult to get a good night's sleep. The ability to concentrate is affected. Feeling like this begins a slide into lower self-esteem. You feel worthless, that you have let people down.

Depressed people are at risk of developing addictions to various substances that offer temporary relief. A common one is having a love-hate relationship with food and/or alcohol. Taken to extremes, depression is a leading cause of suicide.

Dealing with severe depression is beyond the scope of this book; that calls for professional help, the sooner the better for your own sake.

Two: Nature of Loneliness

"The most terrible poverty is loneliness, and the feeling of being unloved." — Mother Teresa.

It's about Disconnection

Loneliness is the feeling of being *disconnected* from others, not necessarily about being physically alone. It is possible to feel alone in a crowd. Being in the company of good friends is one way to feel connected, but there are other ways. The key is to feel yourself to be aligned with a purpose, something that contributes to the greater good. When you become aligned with such a purpose, "connection" becomes more akin to "immersion". It is having a common purpose that you share with other, like-minded people.

Nobel Prize winning playwright George Bernard Shaw, never one to mince words, famously said:

"This is the true joy in life, the being used for a purpose recognised by yourself as a mighty one; the being thoroughly worn out before you are thrown on the scrap heap; the being a force of Nature instead of a feverish selfish little clod of ailments and grievances complaining that the world will not devote itself to making you happy."

Becoming connected with other people is an inevitable consequence of being aligned with a purpose recognised by yourself as a mighty one, as Shaw put it. This is not to imply that you should give up on having friends in the conventional sense. The two scenarios complement each other. When you are with friends, you become a like-minded group which generates a strong sense of being connected to them. In the absence of friends, you can substitute alignment with a *"purpose recognised by yourself as a mighty one"*. It does not have to be one or the other; both is better.

The Need for Acceptance

In human societies and in many animal societies too the need for social connection exerts a shaping influence on behaviour. Our need for acceptance constrains our behaviour in accordance with the behavioural standards of the group. We "pay" for our place in society through our willingness to conform, to "play the game". If we break the rules, the group imposes an escalating range of disciplinary measures. At first, we are ridiculed, then excluded temporarily, then ostracised or expelled altogether. In some societies, non-conformists are put to death.

Social exclusion today is not usually fatal as it was in the evolutionary past, at least not in the physical sense of dying from exposure, starvation or predation, though losing the will to live is a not uncommon result of extreme social isolation. Its no coincidence that the harshest punishment in prison is solitary confinement.

Neuroscientists have mapped the activity in people's brains when they are engaged in a range of activities. It is clearly seen that when people cooperate with each other on worthwhile projects, the 'reward' centre of the brain lights-up. We feel emotionally nourished through that sense of productive connection.

Close cooperation in teams calls for specialised skills. 'Mirror neurones' in our brain promote cooperation, turning a group into a team by helping us to empathise with the other members of the team. To look at people and feel what they are feeling, experience what they are experiencing, albeit in a second-hand way. It is our ability to cooperate that is a primary reason for our success as a species. When we combine empathy with the ability to communicate complex ideas, it is possible to achieve as a team what could not be done by an individual.

Why We Have Big Brains

In the evolutionary sense, our need for social inclusion is one reason our brains have grown large. Anthropologist Robin Dunbar famously proposed his "social brain hypothesis" wherein the relative thickness of the neo-cortex (the recently evolved outer layer of the brain) rose as social groups became larger. This enabled individuals to keep track of the complex set of relationships necessary for stable co-existence.

For example, the Tamarin monkey has a brain size ratio of around 2.3 with a social group of about 5 members. The Macaque monkey has a brain size ratio of around 3.8 and has a much larger social group of around 40 members. Given the brain size of humans, Dunbar estimates we have an expected social group size of around 150 people, which not uncoincidentally is about the size of an extended family or "clan."

People on the Spectrum

With people on the Autism Spectrum, their cognitive resources are redirected away from the default setting of social interaction into areas like mathematical processing, allowing them to perform prodigious feats of calculation but at the expense of being unable to empathise with others or understand the subtle nuances of social interaction.

Seen in the grand context, this is no bad thing. People on the spectrum have contributed disproportionately to human civilisation. In every society there will be those pensive ones who think up new ways, and then those who work with others to bring those idea into existence. We need both kinds. Sir Isaac Newton, for example, was very likely on the autism spectrum. His desire to interact with people was very limited, but his ideas are among the most transformative in the history of science. It was the gregarious Sir Edmond Halley (of comet fame) who ensured Newton's ideas reached a broader audience.

But even the most introverted among us need social connection, though the degree of need will be considerably less than the average person. Everyone has their optimal level to find.

Loneliness is a Signal

A different perspective on loneliness sees it as a signal from our psyche that we have become disfunctionally isolated from our social environment, and that we need to reconnect. Not unlike a low battery needing to be connected to a charger to bring it back to full health.

In the past, that would have been as simple as re-joining our tribe or finding another. Reconnecting today might be more complicated given the greater mobility and ease of modern society. People live far from their families in places where they feel like a stranger in a strange land.

It might also be that the complexities of modern life is creating a degree of anxiety in people generally, leading them to withdraw into the relative safety of their domestic cocoon, reluctant to venture out. These folks will likely compensate by living more of their lives in the on-line world.

There will be various reasons why more people self-describe as lonely, these might be two of them. The fact remains that feeling lonely is a signal to find a way to reconnect with a sense of meaning.

Situations that Cause Loneliness

While the underlying cause of loneliness – disconnection – can occur across many life situations, there are some that entail a higher risk.

New Environments where you don't know anyone, and no-one knows you. Where people are different in the way they dress, the way they talk, the things they do. Where there are different social customs. You feel like the proverbial "*fish out of water*". Moreover, people seem to be established in their friend groups, and the "*no vacancy*" sign looks to be out.

No intimate partner –no-one to share your inner-most thoughts and feelings, someone you can reveal your private self, someone you can trust to not hurt you when you reveal your true self. The need for intimacy exists beyond the need for sex which is more biological than emotional.

Isolation – if you live in a remote area with few or no other people nearby. Ironically its possible to be isolated in a big city with thousands of people nearby. The emotional barriers that people in crowded cities erect to protect themselves from strangers can certainly create a sense of isolation.

My animals – cats and dogs and other companion species that humans have co-habited with for many thousands of years provide much emotional support and do so in a completely non-judgmental way. Our pets have evolved to instinctively want to be with humans and give unconditional love.

Strategies for Reconnection

The chapters that follow outline a series of strategies to help you find your own optimal kind of reconnection. Some of these strategies come directly from evolutionary psychology. Yes we live high-tech lives, but under the skin, down deep in our instincts we are still similar to our distant ancestors. What worked for them can work for us now. If we were somehow able to take a human being living 100,000 years ago, clean them up, give them a shave and good haircut, dress them in modern clothes, they would be indistinguishable from anyone else walking down a city street. Their cognitive abilities would in some ways be superior to our own since not writing things down or recording them means they needed to remember more.

Looking at the world through the lens of evolutionary psychology is a powerful tool for understanding why the world is the way it is, why people behave as they do, and how we can solve some of the more difficult problems that face us.

Three: Sense of Purpose

"He who has a why to live for can bear almost any how."
— *Friedrich Nietzsche*

It's a truism that human beings are *purpose-driven* creatures. It's long been recognized as fundamental to our nature. As Nietzsche commented, we can endure the harshest of conditions provided we have a reason. And the more central to your *raison d'etre* that purpose is, the more motivating and sustaining it is. It is the purpose that gets you out of bed in the morning and puts a spring in your step at the thought of the day ahead.A lonely, depressed person lacks this exhilarating sense of purpose, this elixir of happiness that is excellent for dispelling loneliness.

But what is involved in generating this sense of purpose?

If you can't think of what your purpose is, spend some time thinking deeply about what the best use for your time and energy is. *What is the highest good you can imagine achieving?* Don't sell yourself short, this is when you should dream BIG. Keep asking yourself this question morning noon and night for days or even weeks. I guarantee that eventually your sub-conscious will serve up the answer. It was always there, waiting to be brought to the forefront of consciousness.

A Cause Greater Than Yourself

The philosopher Daniel Dennett put it this way; *find a cause that you consider to be more important than yourself and devote (at least some of) your time and energy to it.* It might seem counter-intuitive that putting something ahead of your own self-interest would generate something good. Experience has shown over many years that doing so creates a powerful sense of purpose. Suspend your disbelief if you have any to put the principle to the test.

Irish playwright George Bernard Shaw was eloquent if not forceful on the point:

"This is the true joy in life, the being used for a purpose recognized by yourself as a mighty one; the being a force of nature instead of a feverish, selfish little clod of ailments and grievances complaining that the world will not devote itself to making you happy.

"I am of the opinion that my life belongs to the whole community, and as long as I live it is my privilege to do for it whatever I can.

"I want to be thoroughly used up when I die, for the harder I work the more I live. I rejoice in life for its own sake. Life is no "brief candle" for me. It is a sort of splendid torch which I have got hold of for the moment, and I want to make it burn as brightly as possible before handing it on to future generations."

In the Past

In the evolutionary environment, our primary purpose was to survive long enough to reproduce. In today's more complicated world, there are many options and opportunities, it is difficult to recognize our priorities, to know in which direction our greatest good might lie.

For some, their purpose in life is still to survive and reproduce, followed by staying alive long enough to watch them grow and enjoy the fruits of grandparenthood.

For others, it is to build a business, or carve out a career in a competitive field. And for still others, it is to take up a cause for the benefit of their community, the nation, or the whole world.

But what if you do not know what your purpose in life is? What if see little purpose in being alive? Maybe you dislike your job but you do it because you need the money.

Here are some practical ways to recognise your purpose in life. Deep down, that purpose is already known to you. You need to dredge down and bring it to the surface of your mind, up from the subconscious.

Banish Delusion

As a coping mechanism for everyday life, it is so very easy to believe things that are not true. These are the little white lies we tell ourselves that over time we come to believe. And it's understandable why we do this, the truth can be a hard pill to swallow sometimes. But facing the truth is the only possible way of moving forwards in our lives. The only avenue of growth.

When you are honest with yourself, your awareness expands, and new horizons open. On the other hand, lack of honesty allows false beliefs or delusions to persist, limiting your ability to distinguish what is real. But honesty comes at a price. There may be some push-back in your outer world; people don't always react well to the truth. Perhaps they are too attached to their own delusions, or perhaps they know what you say is true but do not want to be reminded. But these consequences are relatively short-lived while the benefits are long-lasting. Honesty allows you to *be* the person you are. You also allow those around you to be themselves too.

Many of the problems that life throws our way, particularly the recurring ones, are there because they offer specific lessons necessary for our personal growth. Life serves up what you need, not necessarily what you want. Those experiences will keep coming until you face the truth of them and find a way to process the real meaning. What annoys us about others is an unrecognized and unresolved similar fault in yourself. That annoying person is being the best kind of teacher, even though we dislike them for it. On the other hand, a similarly negative trait in others that we recognize but are not bothered by is an issue you used to have but have now resolved.

Your purpose in life will reveal itself your inherent talents and by those activities that give you greatest satisfaction. Making a thoughtful inventory of your talents is a good thing to do.

The Myers-Briggs personality test (several good free ones available, use Google to find) is a good starting point for understanding your personality type. Apart from a wealth of personality traits, MB will give you a list of typical occupations and pastimes that people with your personality type are drawn to.

Finding your purpose in life is a bit like a torpedo on its way to the target. As it goes, it may stray left or right, but the guidance mechanism corrects its course. Having a sense of purpose keeps you moving in the direction of your ultimate purpose in life, what some your destiny.

Compassion

Compassion is a quality that benefits the beholder in a multitude of ways. One such way is it can help you realize your proper role in life – your purpose.

Compassion is an unconditional love that generates empathy. With empathy you can discern people's needs beyond what they say they want. Have you noticed how what people want and what they need is often not the same thing?

A compassionate mind-set opens you to an awareness of the interconnectedness of everything in Nature. From this powerful awareness comes a growing idea of where your place is in the grand scheme.

Negative emotions like anger and hate are the antithesis and these serve to alienate you from the world around you, making you feel disconnected, alienated. Once this mind-set becomes established, we have the root cause of loneliness.

An angry person can be immersed in a crowd and still feel alone. The compassionate person can be alone on a mountain top and feel a great love and connection with all humanity.

Being mindful

Mindfulness can be a useful tool for discerning purpose. When you are being mindful, you are observing your thoughts moment by moment. Fleeting thoughts that would otherwise be missed can be a strong indication of where your path is laid out.

When a thought comes repeatedly over the weeks and months, there is usually something behind it, but you will not notice unless you are mindfully observing the patterns of your thought.

Mindfulness offers a host of other benefits and is well-worth practicing on your way to self-actualization. The basic principle is that the present moment is the only real place where you can be fully alive. Yes, you can allow yourself to be consumed by thoughts of the past and the future, but those thoughts are not real, not in the way the present moment is real. Past and future are mental constructs that exist only in your mind and nowhere else. The present is when the world outside you exists in all its complexity and potential, the one you negotiate with on your journey through life.

Note: to explore Mindfulness more fully, you might enjoy reading another of my books *Being Mindful* published by Altiora.

Know thyself

Another tool to help uncover your purpose in life is the principle of *know thyself*. The phrase is best known as the exhortation above the portal leading to the famous Oracle of Delphi in ancient Greece. Suppliants visiting the Oracle to ask about their future were advised that the answers were within, and within themselves is where they should search.

Knowing thyself works on the principle of the *macrocosm-microcosm* by which is meant that a person's inner-world is a reflection, in fact a perfect representation on miniature scale of the larger world outside; *"as above, so below"*. You cannot come to know the outer world until you have first come to know that corresponding part of yourself.

It is not the easiest idea to grapple with, that within you, within each of us, is the whole universe, albeit a tiny representation of it. It is tremendously empowering to understand and accept this principle, that all of the answers, all of the resources needed for a great life are already at your disposal waiting to be called on. You just need to know yourself.

So, ask yourself *who am I, what am I, what is good and what is bad for me, where am I going, what is my mission in life?* Asking these questions frequently will be received by your subconscious as questions to be answered. The subconscious will go to work on the problem. Sometime later, perhaps days or weeks later, the answer will bubble up to the surface of your consciousness. Then if you have cultivated mindfulness, you will notice the answer like a buoy that has suddenly appeared in your sea of consciousness.

Four: Community

*"I am of the opinion that my life belongs to the whole
community and as long as I live, it is my privilege to do for it
whatever I can. I want to be thoroughly used up when I die, for the
harder I work the more I live."*
— George Bernard Shaw

In an ideal world, loved ones and good friends would be there when we need them, and conveniently distant when we feel like some "me-time". Those enduring bonds of love and friendship with a small group of special people are the foundation of peace of mind and a sense of well-being. The small group of intimates is embedded within the context of a larger group whom we identify as our "tribe". Today we would probably call this group our "community".

But of course, as many people know all too well, it may not work out that way in the modern world. The simple agrarian life of our ancestors now replaced by an often-alienating urban existence where we find ourselves alone in a vast, uncaring crowd. It recalls Coleridge's Ancient Mariner and *"water, water everywhere, and not a drop to drink."*

In this chapter we explore what a community is and how you can integrate yourself into one without compromising your sense of identity or being unduly influenced by groupthink.

Sense of Identity

Membership of a community contributes greatly to your idea of who you are. And with that idea can come the desire to contribute to the welfare of the community, to act in "pro-social", altruistic ways for the good of the community. We are geared at an instinctive level to feel deep satisfaction when engaged in pro-social behaviour. Our survival at the individual level in the past was directly linked to group survival.

When you have reached some degree of understanding of your place in the larger scheme (as discussed in previous chapters), the choice of which communities to join becomes clear. The people in those communities are those with whom you share common interests and this engenders that feeling of being connected with something larger and more meaningful than you at the individual level.

There is a caveat to this; as social creatures seeking connection with others, we sometimes form relationships with the wrong people driven by the desire to not be alone. From social psychology we know that for better or worse we become like the four or five people we spend the most time with. We instinctively model our behaviour, our speech, our way of thinking on our close associates. It strengthens the bonds of friendship. This is fine when those others are people to help you become a better version of yourself. But we all know people who fall short of those qualities. Just ask the sober alcoholic whose friend circle evaporates when they realize all they really had in common was getting drunk.

We are Already Connected

Communities exist in the larger context of societies. They form a montage, similar to a patchwork quilt that represents a society composed of communities. Moving up a higher scale, societies are located within national borders, collectively forming a nation state. The nation might itself be part of a supra-national entity like the European Union or the United Kingdom or the former Soviet Union. In the past such an entity might have been called an empire. Ultimately though, every one of us is a member of the planet-wide human family, soon to include colonies on the Moon and Mars. We are indeed one family as there has only ever been one race of *homo sapien*. The internet in the past few decades has created a global community.

You already sit at the epicentre of concentric circles. Each circle representing a larger entity in the human hierarchy. Knowing your place in the human family can help you to feel connected to your fellow human beings. After all, we belong to a family that includes every person on the planet.

Let's focus down on the community and societal levels of analysis.

Gemeinschaft & Gesellschaft

To clarify what we mean by "community" the German language sums it up nicely in the concept of *Gemeinschaft (pronounced Ger-mine-sharft), a spontaneously arising organic social relationship characterized by strong reciprocal bonds of sentiment and kinship within a common tradition*, according to Merriam-Webster.

In relation to "society", German expresses the complementary idea of *Gesellschaft (pron. gezell-sharft)* which equates to the structured, regulated environment within which people and communities exist – in other words *society*. Merriam-Webster define *Gesellschaft* as *a rationally developed mechanistic type of social relationship characterized by impersonally contracted associations between persons.*

These two concepts help us to see our place as individuals situated in a community which is situated in a larger society.

In evolutionary times, the extended family, or multi-generational kinship group is the earliest example of a community. Today, the extended family is still the primary community for people everywhere. The instinct to bind together with one's kin is still strong. But this cannot be said of everyone. It could be that study or work has taken you far away, or maybe there is unresolved conflict.

The community phenomenon can also occur among unrelated people, united by a common interest, hobby, occupation or religious belief. In today's connected world, communities of interest are facilitated by the internet and dispersed across the entire planet. There is an amazing diversity of interest groups, some of which have the most minutely specialized interests as their theme. Such groups might have less than a hundred members drawn from a potential pool of billions. If you know what your consuming passion is, that expression of your life purpose, finding a community of interest online is as difficult as doing a series of Google searches.

On the Japanese island of Okinawa where longevity is common, people form mutual support communities (called *moais*) that promote healthy behaviour, the result of which is that Okinawans are among the longest lived people on the planet. It's a good example of the importance of keeping good company.

For some, belonging to a faith-based community is a source of comfort and strength. As a practice, this should not be disparaged in a world where church attendance is dropping. Each to their own.

Five:
Belief in a Higher Power

I am intrigued by different religions and respect them all, but to be honest, I feel the most spiritual when I am doing yoga or looking at an ocean. Being spiritual is feeling a connection with a higher power and knowing that life is about more than just achieving goals. It is about feeling good in the moment.
-- Heather Graham

Religion is a contentious subject in the modern world where church attendance is in decline where people regard it with deep suspicion. People now profess to be atheist, or agnostic or simply "spiritual". To replace the moral guidance once provided by religion, secular ethics has risen to fill the vacuum.

But the reality of religion is that if it did not exist, it would be necessary to invent it. It does exist because it meets pre-existing human needs. This is not to suggest that atheists must necessarily have these needs go unmet. There are secular ways to accomplish this.

This chapter covers what these pre-exiting needs are and how one might go about meeting them, either in a religious or secular way.

To illustrate that religion meets people's needs, take for example religion in Soviet Russia. Marxist doctrine actively discouraged religious observance, dismissing it as a dangerous opiate. The Russian Orthodox Church was thus marginalised. Yet even after 69 years of Soviet rule, the Russian Orthodox Church bounced back with renewed vigour when the Soviet Union passed into history. The fact is, generations of Russians never stopped practicing their religion, they just did it out of sight of the commissars.

Fear the Reaper

It has been said that the *fear of death is the root fear of all fears*. Deep down in places we don't like to go, we know the day will surely come when we slip away into oblivion – what a terrifying thought for a psyche geared for survival! We need assurance that it is not dreamless oblivion that awaits us.

And as the reality of that day looms larger, we look for meaning in the transcendent, a way of believing that promises a continuance of consciousness after the physical body has died. Religious practice or its secular equivalent gives a person a lasting sense of connectedness with a transcendent reality. It is a comforting alternative to eternal dreamless sleep.

Note: The *Tibetan Book of the Dead* is a remarkably clear, matter-of-fact account of what a person can expect after death. I have written a plain English version of this ancient Buddhist text – google on *What Happens When I Die* by David Tuffley.

Religion & Spirituality: The Difference?

At the risk of sounding reductionist, *spirituality* seeks a direct experience of the transcendent, whereas *religion* seeks the same goal but via mediated experience. The mediation is via a priest who makes a bridge between the mundane and the divine. The nature of this role is most clearly seen in the Roman Catholic Pope being called '*The Pontif*' or 'bridge builder' in Latin.

The spiritual person keeps an open mind about how to experience transcendence. They might sample various religious practices to see what works, cherry-picking ideas without becoming committed to the religion from which it came. In looking into various religions, the seeker may notice that similar ideas can be found in different religions, although how those ideas are expressed differs according to the historical period and cultural context.

A sceptical, scientifically-minded person who accepts nothing that cannot be empirically proven can still believe in Physics and the Laws of Nature because those laws have been subject to empirical tests and applied in countless ways with consistent, reliable results. It does not require faith to believe science. But even so, the guiding principles that imbue Physics and Nature with truth do not physically exist. Those principles only exist in the abstract sense. They are not directly observable, only their influence on the behaviour of physical objects can be observed.

Deconstructing Religion

Ninian Smart is a Scottish academic and expert on secular religious studies. He is best known for having identified seven basic practices that are present in all religions. That these common factors exist suggests that the phenomenon of religion is not the product of a culture, but an expression of human instinct.

The seven dimensions are interesting because they seem to be universal across religions, putting a different perspective religion as something that humans have an instinctive need for, rather than supposing it spontaneously arises in societies.

If you are not religious, you can still come to understand what it is that religious people get from their observance and devise alternatives that suit your secular needs. This is will create appropriate conditions within yourself for that sense of being connected to something larger.

Ritual

Ritual has two main functions; to entertain and to reinforce an important message. As a performance, ritual has it all; vocal narrative, visual show, ceremonial robes, music, sound effects, olfactory elements like incense. The location can be a lavishly decorated church interior with soaring ceiling drawing the eye upwards toward heaven. The full gamut of pomp and circumstance.

Ritual is a rich narrative that a person can enter into and feel part of and become immersed in at an emotional level. Christenings, weddings, funerals are all carefully scripted and staged rituals that make it easy for people to feel involved at an emotional level. Since they mark major life events, people tend to remember these occasions and what was said at them. All three of the abovementioned rituals involve a person's family and friends – their clan. In the case of the wedding, the bride and groom are making a public commitment to each other that once made in the presence of those near and dear to them is difficult to break without loss of face.

There are many rituals on the religious calendar; Easter and Christmas being among them. People love the rituals they knew as children, those of Christmas with its gift giving and good cheer. Easter, while marking a tragic event has the compensation of involving large quantities of chocolate.

Rituals for non-religious folk can take any number of secular forms. Most of the rituals that began with religion now have a secular equivalent. People get married, have their new-borns celebrated and give their deceased loved ones a good send-off, all without any mention of God or scripture, heaven or hell.

Narrative & Mythic

The meaning of the term "myth" in common usage has come to imply that something is believed but not true. But myth can also refer to traditional stories, especially those relating to the history of a people or those explaining phenomenon. Myths usually involve supernatural beings or events.

Since humans first learned to talk, we have been recounting stories about how the world and everything in it came to exist. Gods and goddesses beyond the physical world whose favour we earn and whose ire we must placate.

Myths show us our place in the world and gives us some control. Every culture has its creation myths, so myth is a deeply instinctive need possessed by creatures with a big brain who need to understand things.

Using fire was a pivotal event in the proliferation of myths. Gathered around a camp-fire was the ideal place and time to tell and re-tell stories that reinforce social cohesion. The fire protected early humans from marauding predators like bears, big cats and wolves. It gave them warmth and light, cooked their food and engendered a sense of safety. Just as rituals are repeated to reinforce their message, so too are myths. When a message is repeated often enough, people come to believe it literal truth.

There is an incredibly rich source of material to feed one's love of myths to be found in the great literature of the world. For what are great books, but stories written by master story tellers. We could spend many lifetimes reading and revelling in the great works of the English literary canon and still not read them all. Then there translated works from the German, the Russian, the French and many others to choose from.

Experiential & emotional

Our emotional self is the ancient foundation upon which our more recently evolved rational self is laid. It was there in our pre-human ancestors and carried through early human evolution before our brains had the neural infrastructure with which to think logically. It was there before we learned how to communicate verbally.

We share the emotional foundation with animals, as seen in the close bond formed between people and their pets.

Emotion is a kind of universal language; people can empathise with the emotional states of others when they have no common verbal language.

People pride themselves on being logical but while they go through the motions of being logical, much of the time decisions are pre-determined on the basis of how they feel about the situation or persons involved. We see this clearly in elections where an otherwise competent candidate will be defeated because people "just don't like him". That candidate may have been better qualified for the job. The rational thing to do would be elect him, but it is emotion that decides.

The implications of this emotional dimension in religion can hardly be over-stated. It determines what we believe is true about ourselves and the world. Being so deeply embedded is perhaps why it is so difficult to change people's religious belief.

Emotion is generated by ritual and myth; these are the how the emotions of awe, devotion, dread, guilt, mystery, liberation, ecstasy, inner peace, bliss and many others are generated. Each time a person experiences these emotions, it is powerfully reinforced in the psyche and helps to create unshakeable belief.

There are plenty of secular ways for a person to have powerful emotional experiences. Deep immersion in great music, literature and movies are a just a few ways. Great art of any kind is considered great by virtue of its ability to transcend everyday experience and create something extraordinary in the hearts and minds of the beholder. People on the street may not have the ability to create such art themselves, but they recognize it when they experience it, and will pay good money for it.

There are countless ways that we can experience the transcendent without resorting to religion. It is one of life's great pleasures to explore the world of art in a ceaseless search for that magic moment when the art transports.

Social & Institutional

Throughout this book I have emphasised community-belonging. The social and institutional dimension of religion is consistent with all of what has been said on the subject. The issue is not so much whether to belong, but which community to belong to. Preferably it should be one engaged in a pro-social endeavour to get the added benefit of knowing you are contributing to the greater good in some way, big or small.

This is not perhaps an option that will appeal to everyone, but the military offers many opportunities to contribute to the national interest. Like the police at the local level, in a democratic society where the military is not an instrument of oppression, the military fulfils the same role at the international level as the police do domestically. There are malicious people at home and abroad who would harm us if there is no-one to stop them. I'm personally grateful to have them guarding our interests.

Alternatively, there are groups like *Médecins Sans Frontières* or doctors without borders that help people in conflict zones and in places afflicted with endemic diseases.

At a more local level there are a great many community-based groups catering to almost every taste. Everything from bushwalking clubs to Civil War re-enactors, amateur theatre groups, book clubs and every kind of sporting association.

The point is, there are many avenues to be involved with like-minded people and perhaps contribute to society and feel like you are doing something worthwhile with your life.

Ethical & Legal

All communities and societies have behavioural standards that members are expected to follow if they are to remain members. Having rules is not such a bad thing if the standards are reasonable. It allows for the smooth running of that society. Without them, anarchy prevails.

Prescribing behavioural standards has been a prime consideration of religions from the earliest times. It has little to do with spirituality and the hereafter, everything to do with having people get along with each other.

There is a practical reason for this; every well-functioning society has to have them, and people are told what good and bad behaviour looks like. They are also shown what happens to those who transgress.

Over time, every society develops its standards of "moral behaviour" otherwise known as Ethics. Traditionally such standards were taught to the community through attendance at Church on Sunday. As church attendance falls, secular ethics is taking over the role of teaching moral behaviour formerly done by the Church.

Is there a difference between *ethical* and *legal*? There is some overlap of course but what is legal often stops short of what is moral thus creating a grey zone. In business for example, there are practices like exploiting the free labour of interns for many months that are immoral but not necessarily illegal. If business owners think they can get away with a profitable practice that would be considered immoral by community standards, they do it. And every time they make money and get away with it they keep on doing it.

Another example is Tax Evasion and Tax Avoidance. They might *sound* like the same thing, but they are not. *Evasion* is the illegal practice of not paying tax that one is legally obliged to pay, whereas *avoidance* is using legal means to not pay more tax than one is obliged to pay. For some, tax avoidance is no better than evasion, yet there is a difference in a legal sense.

The French sociologist Emile Durkheim famously observed that *when mores are sufficient laws are unnecessary, but when mores are insufficient laws are unenforceable.*

Doctrinal & Philosophical

The doctrinal elements of religion are contained in weighty texts written by theologians and interpreted by other religious scholars. The Old and New Testaments of the Christian Bible together comprise a massive body of doctrine. Other religions likewise have large bodies of doctrine.

It's controversial area because one passage might contradict another. Or a passage may be in direct conflict with current day values, such stoning homosexuals to death, or the giving over of one's virgin daughter to appease an invader.

Religious scholars extract themes to interpret the underlying meaning so as to help people understand the essence of those teachings. These scholars reinforce the role of the priest who job is to mediate between heaven and earth. The formation of doctrine and its philosophical implications is largely an intellectual process engaged in by religious scholars. It may or may not contain errors of logic.

There is a danger that if there is not sufficient separation between church and state, over time elements of political orthodoxy can find their way into religious doctrine. The history of science has many accounts of discoveries being inhibited over concerns that they amount to heresy.

Religious doctrine is one of the most problematic aspects of religion, since it is the work of fallible humans. History has many instances of infallible people being proven wrong about their work.

For non-religious people, doctrine can be formulated using elements drawn for a wide variety of secular sources available to us in the modern world. These include secular philosophies from East and West. One recommended approach is to embark on a program of comparative religions and philosophies, a search for common ground that might exist across traditions. The most obvious example of a common theme found in every religion and some philosophies, the so-called "golden rule" of doing to others what you would have done to you. This principle is expressed in different terms but with the same underlying meaning in all major religions. It's the closest thing to an absolute truth that we can find. It is not a culturally determined value that exists only in a local sense.

I have applied this principle in every aspect of my life over decades. And it continues to serve me well. My grown children have reason to thank me because I made sure when they were little that I treated them the way I would have wanted to be treated when I was their age. They never perceived a double stand, so never had reason to lose faith or be angry in their adolescence. This is a doctrine that I arrived at through careful comparison of sources, not as an article of faith.

Material

This most visible aspect of religion comprises the buildings and artefacts inside them that are imbued with special significance. It includes the priestly vestments and accoutrements that go along with the many rituals. Churches, temples and mosques is where the Divine presence is believed invoked by correctly performed ritual.

The material dimension of religion is best seen in the Christian cathedral, or indeed the mosques of Islam and the temples of other religions. The architecture of these buildings expresses power and glory. The physical presence of the building enters into a dialogue with every observer for as long as that building stands, which, being built to last from the finest materials might be at least a thousand years. And should they be destroyed, an exact replica is built in its place such as when the cathedral of Notre Dame in Paris was badly damaged by fire in 2019.

A good example of the material dimension is the Lutheran cathedral in Berlin, known as the *Berlin Dom*. In a city of grand buildings, old and new, this building is remarkable. Standing before it in the wonderfully named *Lustgarten* one feels very small, in the presence of something transcendant.

The baroque splendour of the Dom is no small thing. I have stood before it and gazed upon it for a long time, waiting until it became a familiar sight, and not so imposing. But its grandeur was not diminished with familiarity. Something about the proportions, the size, the symmetry, the extravagant detail. They combine to speak confidently of the awesome power possessed by the Kings and Queens of

Prussia. And down deep in the crypt, a resting place for their mortal remains.

The interior of the Dom is a feast for the eyes, even the eyes of this 21st Century man who seeks out architectural marvels wherever they are to be found. Designed to draw the eye towards heaven, it is a promise of what awaits the faithful once they pass on from this vale of tears. To dwell among the cherubim and archangels. This vision of heaven in all its splendour would have made a convincing case for people in the past. Seeing the many hundreds attending Sunday service on a freezing morning in January, that message, formulated so many centuries ago, still seems to be working.

The Baroque style of the Dom was a strategy that the Pope used to win back support for Catholicism when the Reformation was sweeping Europe. But there is an anomaly with this church. The main feature of Protestant churches is their austerity, their lack of decoration. A stark contrast to the opulence of your average Catholic cathedral. Yet this is a Lutheran church, it should be austere. And it probably would have been were not the church used by the Prussian royal family.

For non-religious people, the material dimension can be an appreciation of the many fine accomplishments of our modern secular society. Art galleries, museums, grand buildings of all kinds. One does not need to look far in today's world for splendour at the material level.

Six: Exercise

"When it comes to health and well-being, regular exercise is about as close to a magic potion as you can get."
-- Tich Nhat Hanh

We are Adapted for Exercise

Life in the evolutionary environment was very strenuous by modern standards. People walked or ran long distances every day, just to find food and water. In developing areas today, there are still people who must walk five or ten kilometres daily to fetch drinking water, then carry a back-breakingly heavy container back. The people doing this are usually women and children. Contrast with the developed world, where we take clean water on tap for granted.

The human body is adapted to make this kind of herculean effort. We may not think so, not ever having done it, but just as the spirit of the wolf still lives in the most pampered pooch, that ancestral strength is alive and well.

Not too many people have the discipline to perform strenuous exercise on a regular basis. A sedentary life-style contributes to feelings of loneliness because having lots of time to idly sit and think about how terrible one's life is a recipe for unhappiness.

It Should Be Fun

The key then is to find an activity that does not seem like exercise. Something that is more like recreation. In my own case, swimming, walking in Nature and kayaking are my activities of choice based on the innate capabilities I inherited from my parents. Swimming is excellent as one gets older because it is low impact. It does not cause joint problems like running and tennis. Whatever your preference though, set up your day-to-day life to involve enough physical effort to satisfy your body's requirement for movement. It could be walking, running, swimming, chopping wood, cultivating a garden/vegetable patch. Each of these can be a source of great pleasure. The more you enjoy it, the more likely you will continue to do it.

"What you don't use, you lose". With too little exercise the body inevitably goes into a slow decline. Unused muscles are reabsorbed so as not to be a drain on resources. But with reasonable amount of exercise, your body stays in good working order. Flushing your body everyday with plenty of oxygen and clean water is a good foundation. Remember, unless you are disabled you are capable of greater physical feats than you probably think you are.

The Economy of Effort Instinct

There is an evolved instinct in humans to not expend more effort than is necessary. It works against our interests when it comes to exercise. Because people in the evolutionary past were chronically undernourished, often living on the edge of starvation, we evolved what might be called an 'economy of effort' mind-set that conserved energy. We see this instinct today in the modern 'couch potato'.

When economy of effort is practiced by well-fed people, weight gain over time is inevitable. The challenge is to devise a lifestyle that involves moderate, enjoyable, mostly low-impact aerobic activity. It seems like recreation, not a chore.

We are well-adapted to walking. Our ancestors did a lot of walking and loping -- that low-impact gait somewhere between walking and running.

Activity can be complemented by an afternoon nap, a a restorative sleep that rests your body and mind. Cycles of activity and rest throughout the day is a natural way of living, much better than a sedentary life of too much rest and not enough activity, or the opposite situation for some of too much activity and not enough rest.

As a remedy for loneliness, regular, enjoyable exercise has much to recommend it. Exercise causes your body to release endorphins, a natural high that makes you feel good all over and lifts your mood.

So find enjoyable reasons to be active and pursue these activities every day for the rest of your life.

Seven: Nutrition

Looking good and feeling good go hand in hand. If you have a healthy lifestyle, your diet and nutrition are set, and you're working out, you're going to feel good.
-- Jason Statham

Humans, the Supreme Omnivore

What did people eat in the evolutionary environment? Early humans on the savannah were hunter-gatherers who were not averse to dining on what was left after the big cat predators had eaten their fill. One study points to early humans specializing in eating the nourishing bone marrow that their nimble hands and stone tools gave access. Above all, early humans were supreme omnivores, able to eat most things with nutritional value. And when we learned to use fire, a new range of possibilities opened up. Our omnivory has allowed us to spread across the Planet, adapting to habitats everywhere from the equatorial jungles, deserts, grasslands, tropical and temperate forests, all the way to the arctic.

No other creature, with the possible exception of the rat has proved to be quite so adaptable. Most species are limited to a narrow set of environmental conditions and cannot live outside of them. This can be an advantage because it allows for a shorter period of childhood dependency. But humans went the other way. A 13 year dependency period allows the child and adolescent enough time to learn about their environment, rather than relying on instinct as is the case with species with short childhoods that are adapted to a single habitat.

Optimal Diet

While our digestive tract is adapted to consume a wide range of foods, some things are better suited to our digestion than others.

Opinion varies on what the optimum diet for humans might be. Common sense suggests that the best diet is an optimised version of that which people lived on in the evolutionary environment. Over millions of years, our gut evolved to eat nuts, beans, fruit, vegetables, insects and the meat of animals, birds and fish.

Fire has played a major role in our diet. No-one knows how it started. It could have been that we first used fire by taking a burning log, lit by lightning and added more dry wood to make an on-going blaze. The campfire was invented, and what a game changer! Early humans discovered that raw meat tasted better when roasted over a fire or buried in its coals. Not just meat either, so too vegetable, nuts and even insects.

In time, fire enabled early humans to eat things they would otherwise not be able to digest. Too tough or too contaminated with bacteria. Fire pre-digests food, making it digestible, killing harmful bacteria, and improving the taste, all the while giving us the comfort of putting something warm and nourishing into our stomachs.

Strengthen the Bonds of Friendship

Eating with other people is a deeply social activity. When people share a meal, the bonds of friendship are strengthened. This can be useful if you are looking for ways of developing friendships.

We should be sceptical about claims silver bullet diets, there is no such thing. Despite the latest fad diets that come and go, there is still no substitute for the common sense diet of eating what we evolved to eat, except today, we can substitute clean sources of lean protein for wichity grubs and termites.

Eat Less, Exercise More

Maintaining a healthy weight comes down to *eating less and exercising more*. That is eating less fatty, sugary, salty foods while concentrating on lean protein and whole foods.

Highly processed foods, and that is most of what is stocked on supermarket shelves should be eaten in lesser quantities in favour of whole, unprocessed foods. These can either be grown or produced at home in your garden or bought in bulk at low cost. Plenty of water to keep you well hydrated is known to be life-enhancing because it helps rid your body of metabolic by-products.

Caloric Restriction is Healthy

In the past people went hungry quite often. Periodic fasting has been found to promote long-life. It might seem counter-intuitive that going without food would be a healthy practice, but the business of digesting food is an energy-intensive process in itself. Giving your body a break from it every now and then allows it to put energy into repairing the wear and tear inflicted upon it by everyday life. The practice is known as 'caloric restriction'. From studies, it has been concluded that life expectancy can be extended by restricting your caloric intake by around 30%. Nature magazine, one of the most respected scientific journals in the world, discussed the health benefits on ageing primates of adopting a low-calorie diet. It appears that periods of little or no food initiates a protective mechanism in the body that reduces the likelihood of age-related disease.

On the Japanese island of Okinawa where people routinely live to advanced old-age, the practice of caloric restriction has been culturally embedded in the practice of *hari hachi bu* which basically means eat until you're 80% full. Hari hachi bu is a 2,500 year old Confucian-inspired mantra that is said before every meal to remind oneself to not eat to full satiety. One effect of this practice is that less energy is needed to digest a big meal, leaving the person with more energy to exercise with, feeling lighter as they go about their moderate activities.

It is worth remembering that in the past, people typically expended more effort in their daily life. They did this on fewer calories than people consume today. When food was plentiful, our instincts tell us to eat as much as possible, deposit the surplus as reserves of fat to keep us going during the next famine. But today, food is plentiful most of the time and it is all-too-easy to eat too much, exercise too little, and become obese.

Eight: Stress

It's not the stress that kills us, it's our reaction to it.
-- Hans Selye

Manageable Stress is Good

Conventional wisdom has it that stress is a bad thing. But a manageable amount of stress can be a good thing; a challenge to be met and overcome. It is the fact of too much stress that is bad for us. By "too much" I mean more stress than you can constructively manage. So, the objective of stress management is not to eliminate stress, but to minimise its harmful effects on body and mind.

In the evolutionary environment, the insecurities and predatory dangers of life would have been highly stressful. People must have lived in a state of high alert most of the time, ready to spring into action at the first sign of danger. There was the daily struggle to find enough food and drinkable water. There were the external threats from rival groups and predators, and the internal threats from rivals over mate selection and position in the social hierarchy. Little wonder that many individuals did not live beyond their twenties. As Thomas Hobbes famously observed, life in those times was *'solitary, poor, nasty, brutish, and short'*.

Physical stress causes chronic inflammation in the body. Psychological stress leads to traumatic stress disorders of one kind or another. When the negative effects of these is combined, a person's life can be significantly shortened.

But *some* stress makes life interesting. We are built for hard, meaningful work, so we thrive on manageable challenges. Our minds need this healthy stress in the same way that our bodies need exercise. No stress undermines our mental fitness just as no exercise undermines our physical fitness.

Control How You React to Stress

While we cannot avoid stress altogether, we *can* control the way we react to it. For example, take two individuals; same age, education, socio-economic background. One has effective stress-coping mechanisms and the other does not. If each of them was the victim of a street robbery, the one with good coping skills would soon recover, while the other might struggle for years with the effects of post-traumatic stress disorder. If you could listen in to the internal dialogue of each of these people you would likely find that one is positive, the other negative: same stimulus, two different responses. How we respond to the unavoidable stressful events of life is under our control.

As Stephen Covey says in his Seven Habits, *in the space between what happens to you and what you do about it lies your power to choose.* It's a simple idea that can transform your outlook on life if you are accustomed to thinking that life is just something that happens to you. Its true you cannot always control what is done to you, but you *can* control how you react to it. This is the essence of the Stoic philosophy.

Coping Strategies

Well-adjusted people around the world have this in common; ways of neutralising the harmful effects of stress. They have a resilience that allows them to quickly recover from stressful events and regain their equilibrium.

While much has been written on the topic of managing stress; effective management comes down to a few basic principles:

- avoid situations that you know will be stressful,
- understand that you have the power to control your reaction to stress, to not over-react to situations,
- learn relaxation techniques for mind and body, the best of which are deep breathing and meditation,
- being realistic and managing your expectations about how the world *should* be,
- stay in control of your world as far as possible,
- avoid self-medicating with alcohol or other drugs.

Nine: Sense of Humour

A person without a sense of humour is like a wagon without springs. It's jolted by every pebble on the road.
-- Henry Ward Beecher

Laughter Still the Best Medicine

Laughter is a kind of universal human language. It is an expression of an emotional state, and as discussed in a previous chapter, emotion is a universal language of humans and animals too.

Everyone recognizes laughter and most of the time can recognize the emotional state that produces it. And think of the amazing diversity of comedic forms, so many different types of humour producing so many different kinds of laughter. Everything from a quiet chuckle to an uproarious belly-laugh with so much in between.

It feels good to laugh, it is a key element in social bonding. Have you noticed how the world likes people who can make other people laugh?

Laughter Releases Tension

One theory suggests that in the evolutionary environment laughter allowed for the release of tension at the passing of a dangerous situation. Another theory is the "cognitive dissonance" explanation. When you follow a line of thought and suddenly it veers off in a different direction, you experience a momentary confusion that causes a tension which must then be released. This is evident in the punchline of jokes.

Laughter Boosts Resilience

Whatever the origins, the ability to see the humorous side of life is a useful skill that boosts your resilience as well as your enjoyment of life. Good humour calls for an optimistic mind-set that is itself a valuable tonic for loneliness. Laughter brings about healthy physical changes. It strengthens the immune system, releases endorphins to promotes feelings of well-being and reduces pain, improves blood circulation, boosts energy, reduces conflict between people and works to lessen the damaging effects of stress.

Laughter Counters Stress Hormones

A good belly-laugh relaxes your whole body, making it an effective remedy for stress. It has a strengthening effect on the immune system by counter-acting stress hormones. When these stress hormones are present, the immune system is placed under a handicap, making it more difficult to fight infection.

Laughter releases endorphins -- these are naturally released under a variety of circumstances including exercise, excitement (for example laughter), pain, consumption of spicy food, love and orgasm. Endorphins produce an analgesic effect and a feeling of well-being.

Laughter protects the heart, improves the functioning of blood vessels and increases blood flow, all of which helps protect against a heart attack and other cardiovascular problems.

All in all, laughter is a life-affirming act, one which lifts depression and eases the painful effects of loneliness. Find ways to laugh every day, even if it is to watch comedies on TV and the movies.

Ten: An Attitude of Gratitude

"Gratitude is the healthiest of all human emotions. The more you express gratitude for what you have, the more likely you will have even more to express gratitude for." — *Zig Ziglar*

Being complacent, having a sense of entitlement or taking the circumstances of one's life for granted has a distinctly corrosive effect on a person's sense of well-being. It can create resentment towards those who have more. And it is all too easy to acquire these mind-sets in the modern world.

Now I'm not saying there is anything wrong with having a good standard of living, rather that we should not take it for granted because doing so leads to feeling envious towards those who apparently have it better than we do. The grass will always seem greener on the other side.

Gratitude is the natural remedy. Cultivating a grateful mind-set can have a very positive effect on how we relate to the world and the people in it.

Gratitude is Transformative

For many, gratitude is really just about being polite and saying thank-you when someone does something for you. But it goes far beyond that to a general knowing of how much is enough to meet your needs, and the related point of recognizing, not overlooking, the many good things already in your life. No matter how bad things get, they could always be worse. Better to focus on that orientation to life than the opposite one of being resentful that things are not better.

Gratitude once established as a mind-set opens you to child-like wonderment at the world. When you take nothing for granted, and expect very little, everyday things take on marvellous new meaning.

The world is generous to those who are grateful, have you noticed? The person who complains about their life; what they have or do not have is closing the door to greater abundance. Life does not reward this attitude with greater blessings, quite the opposite.

Live Each Day As Though It Is Your Last

As a thought exercise, imagine that today is your last day on earth. How very precious does every minute of life now seem? I have come close to being killed on two separate occasions much earlier in my life. Once in a climbing accident, the second in a horror smash on the highway. Both times it seemed that death was inevitable, I could see no possible way out. But almost miraculously I was spared.

Though these events happened many decades ago, it has left me with the legacy that every day of life is a precious gift that I am grateful to have. I live each day as though it is my last, I live it to the fullest so that if I were to go today, my last thought would not be one of regret.

Live as though you will die today but plan as though you will live forever.

Eleven: Stimulate Your Brain

Neuroscientists studying the human brain have made a startling claim; *our brains are the most complex structure ever to have existed on planet Earth*. Little wonder that it is estimated we only use a small proportion of its total capability in our day to day lives.

Recent work in the nature of intelligence by Harvard professor Howard Gardner points to the way that intelligence can be expressed in up to nine different ways. It is not difficult to see how each of these ways would have been an advantage in the evolutionary past. But what is interesting today is how to develop each of these in our own lives to become a much more well-rounded person. We can expand our repertoire of capabilities greatly and in so doing banish loneliness as a thing of the past.

This chapter focuses down on these intelligences and offer ways you can develop that intelligence in your own unique way. This is a tonic for loneliness in several ways; it's a therapeutic approach that does not seem like therapy but a form of self-improvement that cures loneliness as a by-product.

If there is unused capacity in the human brain there is potential to cultivate our cognitive abilities beyond their current level. Neural plasticity, or the ability re-route or forge new neural pathways is possible, but it requires considerable effort. It may not come easily, but the pay-off is worth the effort.

Multiple intelligences

Harvard professor Howard Gardner is well-known in academia for his work on multiple intelligences. Since its emergence in the 1980's, Gardner's work is still somewhat controversial, yet there are those in the field who believe it contributes significantly to a more comprehensive understanding of the nature of intelligence, than that of the standard IQ test.

The nine types include; *Naturalistic intelligence, Bodily-kinaesthetic intelligence, Linguistic intelligence, Interpersonal intelligence, Spatial intelligence, Logical-mathematical intelligence, Musical intelligence, Intra-personal intelligence, and Existential intelligence.*

We have all nine types, although one or two are likely to dominate. As you read about the various types, you might gain some insight into where your strengths lie and which ones could be enhanced to achieve a more balanced profile of intelligence.

A person well-endowed with certain types of intelligence may have done poorly at school with curriculums based on the standard IQ assessment. They might have the opinion of themselves that they are not very bright. For example, someone with high *Intra-personal* intelligence would probably not engage well with formal school curriculums, even though that person has an intuitive understanding of the concepts in the curriculum. Such a person is no less 'intelligent than the student whose native abilities suit them well to perform the set curriculum. They are not the same, but equal in the larger sense. Standardized IQ tests are an indication of what society values in people and indicates their potential in the labour market of a hundred years ago.

It is the all-rounder who is more valuable today in the age of intelligent machines. A hundred years ago, people good at maths were in demand, today computers are used for maths intensive jobs. It is the creative, unorthodox problem-solver who is in demand today. Someone with good communication and team-work skills.

Aim for a balanced profile

The potential for all nine types are present in everyone, but these are manifest to different degrees. As we will see in the discussion of each, they all fulfilled a survival function in the evolutionary past. In way they a set of tools that our ancestors used to meet the survival challenges that faced them in everyday life.

Most people are well-developed in two or three types, with the remainder being somewhat un-developed. Make it your business to cultivate your under-developed types and open up whole new horizons of possibilities. A person good at maths might not be particularly good at communicating, or so they think. A good communicator might not have developed their mathematical abilities. But both can nonetheless work on their underdeveloped sides and become good all-rounders.

Bringing multiple intelligences to bear on your day to day activities boosts your creative potential. It is to bring a multi-faceted tool-kit to bear on a situation rather than relying on a single tool.

Naturalistic intelligence

Naturalistic intelligence is sometimes described as being 'Nature smart'. It is knowing at a feeling level that everything in the natural world is connected to everything else. Given the tremendous complexity and rich detail of the natural world, being able to take a comprehensive view requires a powerful form of intelligence.

Naturalistic intelligence must clearly have been an advantage in the evolutionary past. It may have been the first kind of intelligence that humans had. Hunters-gatherers needed it to understand the subtle attributes and rhythms of the natural environment.

People with highly-developed naturalistic intelligence probably see themselves as being an integral part of Nature, not a separate entity as might be perceived by the many. Naturalistic intelligence is useful for being Nature and operating comfortably.

Beyond the practical, there is a more esoterically developed form seen in the *Shaman* figure. Shamans perceive the abstract realm beyond the physical world. The abstract might be thought of at the realm of spirit, which can be thought of "essence" in this context. Shamans in various forms are found in tribal cultures around the world. It illustrates a highly developed form of naturalistic intelligence albeit one that has been intensified through the use of entheogenic substances, which are not recommended here.

In the modern world, people with advanced naturalistic intelligence are leading the environmental movement. There are many notable people who might be mentioned in this regard. Sir David Attenborough, Rachel Carson, Charles Darwin, John James Audubon, Jacques Cousteau, David Suzuki, Jane Goodall, Steve Erwin, Neil deGrasse Tyson are all examples. Their work has brought an unparalleled appreciation of the natural world to billions of people who sense the importance of cultivating this form of intelligence.

Action exercise: to develop Naturalistic intelligence, it is as simple as establishing a strong connection with Nature. So, spend time in Nature, preferably alone. Go somewhere away from civilization, clear your mind and patiently allow Nature to communicate its subtle messages to you. It may take a long time before your mind quietens enough to perceive the subtle communication. Impatience and the hunger for sensation and entertainment that people in the developed world have learned works against this process. You must slow down and be alert to the subtle flow of information. Lawrence Durrell, in his book Spirit of Place describes how to create this connection with Nature:

"It is a pity indeed to travel and not get this essential sense of landscape values. You do not need a sixth sense for it. It is there if you just close your eyes and breathe softly through your nose; you will hear the whispered message, for all landscapes ask the same question in the same whisper. 'I am watching you -- are you watching yourself in me?' Most travellers hurry too much...the great thing is to try and travel with the eyes of the spirit wide open,

and not too much factual information. To tune in, without reverence, idly -- but with real inward attention. It is to be had for the feeling...you can extract the essence of a place once you know how. If you just get as still as a needle, you'll be there."

Bodily-kinaesthetic intelligence

Kinaesthetic intelligence is the ability to process information physically through hand-eye coordination and strategically controlled body movement. Its how skilfully a person moves their body as an instrument.

Athletes and sportsmen and women of all descriptions, dancers, actors, martial arts practitioners, indeed any occupation that requires coordinated physical activity all rely on bodily-kinaesthetic intelligence.

It is perhaps ironic that people with this kind of intelligence are not normally thought of as being intelligent. Not when they may not be good at maths nor articulate in speech. They are regarded as being 'good at sport (or dancing etc)' and little else. Olympic medal winners can all be said to possess advanced kinaesthetic intelligence; superb physical fitness alone does not win medals.

Advanced kinaesthesia needs significant cognitive resources to manage the coordination of the hundreds of muscles that move the body. This neural activity is happening in a different part of the brain from where mathematics, logic, and linguistic thinking occurs.

Beyond the obvious advantages of being able to control one's body, this form of intelligence is also able to make you a more effective communicator at the non-verbal, body language level. By some estimates, 70% of the meaning conveyed in person to person communication is in the non-verbal category. Using good body language to convey one's message is an aspect of bodily-kinaesthetic intelligence.

Like Naturalistic intelligence, bodily-kinaesthetic would have given an individual an advantage in the evolutionary environment. During the hunt, the kinaesthetic attributes of agility and directional accuracy with launched weapons would have been very helpful in the struggle to survive.

Action exercise: to develop Bodily-kinaesthetic intelligence, the challenge is to discover the particular form of physical activity you have an aptitude for and concentrate on developing it. Many people with highly developed intellectual skills have little or no interest in physical activity. At school they were compelled to participate in sport and probably hated it.

For example, in my own case I was made to play Rugby football and did poorly at it. My body does not like to run, nor does it like being crash-tackled. It does like to swim and as it turns out, it has aptitude for it. Over time I developed into a marathon swimmer.

Swimming in the ocean is an example of how I develop both Naturalistic and Bodily-kinaesthetic in the same activity. My body also likes to walk, and hiking through environments of great natural beauty is another way that I develop both naturalistic and bodily-kinaesthetic dimensions of intelligence.

We are all good at something on the bodily-kinaesthetic dimension. None of us are so far removed from our evolutionary roots that our physical skills have deserted us, regardless of how rusty they have become through disuse. The challenge is to accept that this is true and reject the mistaken belief that there is nothing physical that you are good at. Find that 'something' and discipline yourself to perform it regularly. It needs to be enjoyable though. If it seems like hard work, you will find it difficult to sustain over a long period. There are obvious health benefits too in adopting a regular exercise habit.

Mindful walking may be the best option for you. Going for long walks in which you are fully and consciously present in the moment is one of life's simple pleasures. The more present you are, the more enjoyment you will get from this simple activity. It will take considerable discipline to not think about issues that may be troubling you, to not stew over past wrongs or worry about the future. Forget them all, at least for a time, and experience in vivid detail the place you are in at every moment. It is a form of walking meditation. Such a walk could be as short as half an hour, or as long as several hours. Remember, our ancestors walked long distances on an almost daily basis. Your body still has that capability (provided you are not disabled, of course).

If you do happen to be disabled, and walking is not possible, your therapist will be happy to suggest forms of activity that are suitable for your condition.

Linguistic intelligence

People with linguistic intelligence are skilled writers and speakers who have a deep understanding and love of language. Language is a syntactically-governed string of symbols that we readily absorb as children. The human ability to absorb the complexities of language is truly remarkable, being far more advanced that our primate cousins.

People assume that the purpose of language is to communicate with other people, but that is only half true. Communicating with *yourself* is also an intriguingly important use of language; it is for both *inter*-personal and *intra*-personal communication. With this latter form, language is an indispensable tool of thought. Without it, we are severely limited in *what* we can think about and *how* we think about it.

George Orwell illustrated this in his novel *1984*. The totalitarian government in this landmark book went to some effort to limit people's vocabulary down to a handful of words. They were unable to think any thoughts outside of the established political orthodoxy.

Advanced linguistic intelligence endows the ability to devise communication strategies to meet challenges and achieve their ends. This ability in our evolutionary past gave groups to operate as teams, to co-ordinate their efforts to do things they could not have done alone. An example would be the hunting band of ten individuals coordinating their movements to bring down an animal larger than any one of the individuals. Successful sporting coaches today know how to engender the same effective teamwork.

Linguistic intelligence is a key component of leadership, the essence of which is to communicate a compelling vision of how the future could be to create the enthusiasm needed to make it so.

In classical Greek times, the importance of linguistic intelligence was well-recognised in the practice of Rhetoric. The principles identified during classical times have yet to be improved upon in the modern world. We can see them at work in the advertising industry today.

Some would argue that linguistic intelligence is an innate quality that you have or don't have – not something that can be learned. Those old Greek rhetoricians would disagree, as would many researchers today. People with even a modest degree of linguistic intelligence have been improving their abilities through the learning of communication skills and the systematic practice of those skills until they become second nature.

Action exercise: to develop Linguistic intelligence, feed your mind daily with the best quality material you can get your hands on. Fortunately, the great literature of the world is readily accessible for little or no cost, given that much of it is out of copyright now. You can readily obtain great literature from your local library, or download a digital copy to your eBook reader.

When Earnest Hemingway was asked which writers had influenced him, he replied with a list of twenty or more names of earlier great writers. He spent years reading and digesting the work of dozens of masters and this was the foundation for his own work. This is a commonly heard story in the world of writing. Spend an hour a day reading the work of the great writers. You may need to downgrade the importance of watching TV to make room for this exercise, but it will most definitely be worth it in terms of becoming a better communicator.

Take your time with this kind of reading. Let the pattern of words and their rhythm sink in deeply. Savour the words and develop a love for them. They will love you back, become your friends. They will come to your aid when you need them, become a trusted ally. Does this sound fanciful? Perhaps, but ask any writer how they feel about words and you will hear a similar story. You do not need to be a writer to get benefit from this exercise.

Read something good every day and over time, you will improve incrementally. After a year you will not a real difference. After ten years, you will have become a more effective communicator than most of the people you know.

Interpersonal intelligence

Interpersonal intelligence governs the ability to take appropriate action based on perceptions of the emotions, motivations, intentions and desires of others. For a social species like we humans, this type of intelligence calls for empathy and well-developed communication skills. People on the autism spectrum are challenged in this regard. With autism the cognitive resources usually deployed to interpersonal intelligence service one of more of the other forms of intelligence.

Most primate species exhibit high degrees of sociability and this ability has been linked to how developed is the pre-frontal cortex (PFC) where higher thought occurs. Humans have the most developed PFC of all primates which allows us to aggregate in relatively large social groupings of around 150. Not coincidentally, this is roughly the size of a Neolithic village. 150 is about the maximum number of people any one person can keep track of, given the thousands of possible relationship permutations.

Interpersonal intelligence helps us negotiate the dynamics of social relationships and ultimately how to live in large social groupings with a minimum of conflict. Empathy is a prime ingredient of interpersonal intelligence. For empathy to function, we need to have our 'mirror neurons' working. These allow us to experience, by proxy, what another person is experiencing; to develop what psychologists call a theory of mind about what another person is thinking.

Action exercise: to develop Interpersonal intelligence and fire up those mirror neurons, cultivate the foundational attribute of empathy. Despite the cultural differences between people around the world, we are all human under the skin. There is only one race of humans, one group known as Homo Sapiens. Regardless of appearances and cultural practices, the way you think and feel in a given situation is likely to be much the same as anyone anywhere would think and feel in a similar situation.

When you come to accept that other people are essentially the same as you at the foundational level, a subtle but powerful shift in perception occurs. You come to see them in a different light; you can imagine yourself in their situation and know empathically how they must be feeling. This mind-set requires you to set aside the 'us and them' thinking that has pervaded our evolutionary past. When the world is polarised into the categories of 'us' as in our little group, and 'them' as in everyone else, those outsiders are potential enemies who might harm us. It is very difficult to relate empathically to 'them'.

Widening your 'circle of care' as the ethicist Peter Singer calls it is a way to change the world. We are much less likely to go to war and want to harm someone who we have included in our circle of care. That circle, for many people, extends no further than their family and close associates. But if one gradually widens the circle to be more and more inclusive, in time there will be no 'them' only 'us'.

Spatial intelligence

Spatial intelligence solves spatial problems like navigation, visualization of three-dimensional objects from different angles in space, recognizing faces or scenes, and the observation of easily-overlooked details. When you can see things clearly in your mind's eye you can make prototypes in your imagination and test them.

Spatial intelligence probably evolved way-finding in the evolutionary environment, noting the presence of useful features like water sources, food, predators and natural hazards.

Spatial intelligence is the skill used by architects and town planners to design the buildings and cities we live in, the transport networks as well as the myriads of designed objects in the world.

Every made object in the world began in somebody's imagination. Spatial intelligence has created the modern world and everything in it.

Action exercise: to develop spatial intelligence, cultivate an active interest in a design discipline of your choosing. If you are not sure, then Architecture would be a good starting point.

Architecture is a spatial language, it is not just about designing functional spaces. I do not mean the technical terminology used by architects to do their work. Every piece of architecture, every building is making a non-verbal statement to the world and keeps on making it for as long as it stands. The building communicates the values and aspirations of the person or institution that paid for it to be designed and built. For example, a wealthy man may build himself a grand mansion which says to the world, I am a man of wealth and taste; this is my legacy to the world. The grand country houses of the British and European aristocracies are all making this some version of this statement in a variety of architectural styles.

King Louis XIV of France built perhaps the grandest palace of all in Versailles. It had the practical purpose of housing the Royal Court, but it also had the important task of impressing visitors with Louis' wealth and power. It was a foolish nobleman anywhere who built a bigger palace than the King himself had.

In England, when Henry VIII saw that Hampton Court as built by Cardinal Wolsey, perhaps the second most powerful man in the country was more impressive than Henry's nearby palace, the king simply took it from Wolsey and called it his own. Wolsey had been most unwise and suffered enormous financial loss as a result.

Baroque architecture is seen all over Europe in cathedrals and palaces and public buildings. This architectural form was an attempt to win back support for Roman Catholicism during the Reformation when Matin Luther and the various Protestant movements across Europe resulting in too many people leaving the Catholic church. Baroque was a splendid glimpse of heaven, a promise to the faithful of what awaited them in the next life if they remained faithful. The austere, unadorned Protestant church interiors offered no such glimpse of paradise. Even today, the splendour of some Baroque edifices is still truly breath-taking to the modern eye accustomed to wonders. Imagine how impressive it must have been several hundred years ago to people accustomed to living in squalid, cramped houses.

Visit any city that was once an imperial capital (London, Paris, Rome, Madrid, Berlin) and you will see many buildings that still express the power of an empire that has now passed into history. Empires are an agglomeration of multiple nations, so imperial cities go one better than national capitals in the grandeur of its architecture.

All of this is clearly visible to a visitor walking around. Try to learn the language of architecture so that you can walk around these cities, looking at the buildings and know the statement that began as a thought in someone's mind hundreds of years ago. It is a rewarding pass-time, and one which enriches the travel experience greatly. When you visit a new city, wander about and read the story that its buildings tell.

The TV documentaries of the architectural historian Dan Cruickshank are very good at helping you along with interpreting the language of architecture and come to appreciate the many different architectural forms found around the world.

Logical-mathematical intelligence

Mathematical intelligence has long been considered a primary indicator of intelligence.

Mathematics is a language, though people do not usually recognize it as such. It is the language of Physics and it describes the universe, those abstract principles underlying Nature. Every other language used by humans is culturally based, but Mathematics is universal.

Were it to happen that an advanced civilization was discovered elsewhere in the universe, they would certainly have their own version of mathematics which would in all likelihood share the same concepts (like Pi) because the same laws of Nature and physics apply everywhere.

Maths began with the practical need to keep a record of quantities, whether it was how many times some significant event had occurred or how many items had been accumulated and perhaps traded. It would have started with addition and subtraction. Over time, with the need to solve ever more complex problems, arithmetic came to include multiplication and division. Over time, the various sub-disciplines emerged including algebra, geometry, analysis, topology, combinatorics, and number theory.

The cognitive skills required for mathematical thinking include being able to calculate, quantify, and think hypothetically in an abstract way. A mathematician sees relationships and connections and uses abstract, symbolic thought, plus sequential reasoning skills to solve problems.

Action exercise: to develop Logical-mathematical intelligence, a good place to begin for those of us who are not particularly good at Maths is to cultivate your logical/rational faculty. Logic is a foundational aspect of Maths. The ability to think logically is an aspect of higher cognition, a function of the more recently evolved part of the brain.

So cultivate the habit of thinking logically about situations that you might otherwise have made an emotionally-based decision on. Think the matter through, take the time and make the effort to think logically, resisting the powerful temptation to fall back into emotionally based thinking. By doing so, you are activating these more highly evolved parts of your brain.

Your lizard brain (that primitive, reptilian brain that still resides in humans) will ridicule this approach, heaping scorn upon it in an effort to preserve the status quo. Do your best to ignore this, reminding yourself that you were born with faculties that you have not yet become aware of, and this effort is awakening those faculties, forging new neural pathways in your brain. That can be quite uncomfortable.

Musical intelligence

> *"If music be the food of love, play on."*
> *Shakespeare, 12th Night.*

If Maths is the language of Physics, then music is surely the language of emotion. As a way of communicating at the level of feeling, music has no parallel. The closest anything comes is lyrical poetry which gains much of its power form the musical rhythms in which it is expressed.

Music abounds in Nature. One need look no further than the dawn chorus of bird-song in any forest anywhere in the world. Humans are by no means the only species that expresses itself musically, though for sheer diversity of musical expression, humans have no equal. In the courtship rituals of some birds, it is the complexity and virtuosity of the male's music-making that is used by the female to gauge intelligence and therefore his suitability to father her off-spring.

Every human culture has some form of musical expression which is a unique expression of that culture is. Listening to that music opens a window into the soul of that culture, giving insights that can be obtained no other way.

In our evolutionary past, the language of emotion was probably the language with which early humans expressed themselves. Their tonally expressed utterances would have been similar to those of our primate cousins. Over time this developed into our ability to sing. The area of the brain that governs singing is not the same as that which is concerned with speech. We know this because people with a stuttering speech impediment can nonetheless sing as fluently.

Musicians possess a form of eloquence no less powerful than that of the great rhetorical speakers. In its most elevated forms, music seems to enter the realm of the transcendent, the place where great ideas are to be found. Only those who have never experienced it would dispute that great music has a soul and possesses the ability to transport a listener to a transcendent plane.

It is rare to find someone who claims to not like *any* music. The average person may not have the ability to compose music like the great composers, but they can still *appreciate* that music. That appreciation requires a degree of musical intelligence.

The writer Kurt Vonnegut once commented that *"Music is, to me, proof of the existence of God. It is so extraordinarily full of magic"*.

The cognitive requirements for musical intelligence include the ability to discern pitch, rhythm, timbre, and tone to a high level of awareness. It is evident in composers, conductors, musicians, vocalists, and appreciative listeners.

Action exercise: *to develop Musical intelligence, cultivate an attitude that all music has merit, not just the kind you like. All music deserves to be listened to at least once, even the kind you do not like.*

Actively broaden your musical tastes, seeking out and listening to musical genres that you previously avoided or have not heard before. There is an astonishing variety of music in the world. Every culture has produced its own unique form of music. Much of that music still survives in the world and is available on the internet via Spotify, Google Play, YouTube and others.

Because music is largely about the expression of emotion, much of what you listen to beyond your favourites will produce an uncomfortable sensation that will make you want to switch it off. After all it is assumed that listening to musical should be pleasant, otherwise why would you do it? But I'm suggesting that you do it to open your mind to previously unknown musical influences to develop your musical intelligence. You can experience what people in other parts of the world feel deeply. The musician wants to share that experience with you if you would let them. Accept their gift with gratitude. You can think of it as a form of travel that you do not need to leave home to experience.

As an extreme example, do a Google video search on 'death metal'. What comes up is going to seem repulsive to most people with its demonic vocals and wall of harsh sound. Without judging it, ask yourself what this music is really saying? It is expressing the alienation and angst that some people are feeling. The music is a window into their tormented world. You do not have to like it to empathise and understand their world-view. Look for something good in it. In the case of death metal it may be that the music is all that stands between a deeply unhappy teenager and suicide. They will not always feel this way. They just need to get through it.

Then Google on 'Bach violin concerto' and choose one from the list. What you now hear could scarcely be more different from death metal. You are hearing music that expresses devotion to a divine ideal, sacred music made to be listened to in a sacred space. It is looking to the bright light of divine eminence and imagining paradise. Death metal is looking into the dark sulphurous pits of hell where souls in torment writhe. Now here's the important part. Try to make your opinion of these two very different genres as neutral and judgment-free as possible. Try to understand what the music is really saying without making value judgments. Both types of music are expressing something real about the human condition, albeit at opposite ends of the spectrum.

If you can accomplish this feat, then all of the music in between these extremes will become more accessible to you, and your musical intelligence will have been enhanced. So begins a lifetime enjoyment of music made possible by this new dimension of appreciation.

Intra-personal intelligence

'Intra' meaning 'within' refers to that form of intelligence oriented towards looking within oneself to observe and analyse thoughts, motivations, intuitions, etc. It is an introspective orientation that reflects upon strengths and weaknesses, to play with ideas, and examine one's motivation. Albert Einstein had highly developed intra-personal intelligence.

In classical Greece, intra-personal intelligence was highly valued. The Oracle of Delphi's famous exhortation to 'know thyself' was directed towards developing intra-personal intelligence. To know the outer world, it is necessary to first know one's inner world. Socrates whose work laid the foundation for all Western philosophy went so far as to assert that *the unexamined life is not worth living* -- a ringing endorsement for intra-personal intelligence.

People with high intra-personal intelligence recognises that their inner world is their primary reality, with the outer world their secondary reality. The knowledge and wisdom derived from intra-personal intelligence can be generalised and used to good effect in the outside world. It is not an entirely inward-looking practice, though it would appear that way to people of a more extraverted nature.

In our evolutionary past, intra-personal intelligence would have been responsible for many of the breakthrough innovations achieved by our ancestors.

Action exercise: to develop Intra-personal intelligence, learn how to meditate. Meditation at its simplest is best described as **heightened awareness without the mental chatter***. Meditation basically quietens the mind so that you can calmly observe it.*

With our restless minds demanding entertainment, meditation is difficult. The method outlined here is the basis of many meditation methods. It is simple to learn, though perhaps it will take a lifetime to master.

Begin by sitting comfortably and begin to breathe rhythmically*. Sit with spine straight but in a way that will not induce sleep. Breathe deeply, from the diaphragm, in through your* *nose and out through your mouth. If you get horizontal, or too comfortable, sleep will not be far away. Sleep is not meditation. Sleep is unconsciousness, absence of awareness.*

Focus your conscious awareness on the place immediately behind the centre of your forehead, *the so-called Third Eye, the place where your highest awareness resides. Imagine your attention is a focused beam of light that illuminates and energises your highest awareness in its home, the Third Eye (centre of your forehead, just above the bridge of your nose). Generate a strong desire to bring the highest awareness into your everyday awareness. You know that this place is the centre of your inner world, your most sacred place and the very heart of who you are. You know you have succeeded with this step when you have a strong feeling of being centred.*

While maintaining this feeling of centredness, allow your attention to expand outwards in all directions. *The focussed beam of light now becomes a beacon of light radiating out in all directions. Expanding your awareness outwards like this should give you a sense of spaciousness, ease and lightness. The centering and expansion can proceed almost simultaneously and should involve no further effort beyond the effort to focus and then radiate your attention in the way described. It is not something you should try to do, or force yourself to do. You allow it to happen. It is a natural state of awareness that existed in our distant ancestors before we developed egoic thinking. This spacious but centred awareness is a natural state of mind that you are allowing to become re-established in yourself, not something new that you have to work to establish.*

After centering your awareness and then allowing it to expand outwards, continue to **consciously breathe deeply and** *rhythmically. Concentrate your awareness on the in-breath without engaging in any mental commentary. Simply be aware of the breath as it comes in, and be likewise aware as it goes out, all the while remaining centred, aware and thoughtless. This is the essence of meditation.*

*You can count **sub-vocally on the out-breath** up to a certain number of breaths, (say 50). Or you can set a timer to remind you when ten minutes has passed. Ten minutes is a good duration to begin with. Do the ten minutes for two weeks or so until it becomes well-established, then gradually increase the duration up to 30 minutes over the weeks that follow.*

*Your goal should be to meditate in this way for up to **30 minutes, twice a day**. It is good to begin your day with a meditation session. Likewise end the day with a session in the evening not long before bed-time.*

Existential intelligence

Existential intelligence is the ability to see the 'big picture', to understand people and the world in which they live. This form of intelligence is found in self-actualising people who are moving towards a fuller expression of their human potential.

They are ready to engage with the really big questions; *who am I, why am I here, what is my purpose in life?* The potential for existential intelligence exists in everyone, though it is unlikely to be expressed when the more basic aspects of one's life remain a problem to be solved.

Existential intelligence uses the foundation laid by well-developed intra-personal intelligence. A person must be comfortable in their own skin and have arrived at a good functional understanding of the world and their place in it. Once this is achieved, what else is there left to do but ponder the big questions?

Action exercise: to develop Existential intelligence, a solid foundation of the preceding eight types should first be laid. It is not strictly necessary to be highly accomplished in all eight preceding types before embarking upon the ninth, though it is ideally the case. You will have a balanced repertoire of cognitive abilities that will be excellent for solving whatever problems and achieving whatever aims you might have in life.

Existential intelligence might also be described as self-actualization. Existential intelligence could also be described as the search for spiritual meaning, or transcendence.

Twelve: Bringing it Together

You will have noticed that this is not the average "how to" manual. It takes an holistic approach the understanding the causes and remedies for loneliness. It gives you a range of practical ideas for how you can cultivate a positive mind-set in relation to solitude and have an interesting inner life.

Of course, I am not suggesting you should become a recluse. There will be opportunities to socialise and it would be wise to take advantage of them provided the company will not drag you down through indulgence in addictive behaviours. When you have the chance to spend quality time with people whose company makes you a better person, you should take it and enjoy the benefits. But when this is not possible, it's good to know how to be alone with yourself and be happy about it. Seeking company simply because you do not want to be alone is not a good enough reason. Some 'friends' are really just acquaintances who want company while they indulge their vices.

One of the major messages of this book is that an excellent remedy for loneliness is to discover a greater sense of purpose in life and taking action on it. From this will come feelings of belonging and connectedness with something larger and more meaningful than yourself.

To assist you in finding your purpose and pursuing it is the sharpening up of your cognitive abilities. Gardner's work on multiple intelligences has much to offer people seeking to enhance and round-out their overall ability to think and act. Intelligence comes in nine modalities; the ideal situation is where you regard these as a kind of cognitive tool box such that when presented with a situation or problem to be solved you can select whichever modality or selection of modalities is going to be best for that situation. This has obvious advantages over just using your most highly developed mode for ever situation. As the old saying goes, *if all you have is a hammer, everything looks like a nail.*

Regardless of what we you told at school about what you're good at, how smart you are, what you'll amount to, understand that this is not cast in concrete. Through understanding and the miracle of neuroplasticity you can re-program your way of thinking and rid yourself of negative perceptions that are holding you back and probably contributing to your feelings of loneliness.

All the very best,

David Tuffley

The End

References

Cacioppo, J. T., Fowler, J. H., & Christakis, N. A. *Alone in the crowd: The structure and spread of loneliness in a large social network.* Journal of Personality and Social Psychology.

Cacioppo, J. (2008, Nov. 3). *John Cacioppo on How to Cope with Loneliness.* Source: http://bigthink.com/johncacioppo/john-cacioppo-on-how-to-cope-with-loneliness

Gardner, Howard, 2008, *Multiple Intelligences:* New Horizons, Basic Books, New York.

Loneliness affects how the brain operates. (2009, Feb. 19). Science Daily. Source: http://www.sciencedaily.com/releases/2009/02/090215151800.htm

Swami V, Chamorro-Premuzic T, Sinniah D, Maniam T, Kannan K, Stanistreet D, Furnham A. *General health mediates the relationship between loneliness, life satisfaction and depression. A study with Malaysian medical students.* Social Psychiatry Epidemiology, February 2007.

Printed in Great Britain
by Amazon

Winkton Abbey;

ISBN- 9781079412123

www.jonathanwedge.com

NEVER GIVE UP AND YOU WIN

£1000 TREASURE HUNT

In July 2019 **£1000** was **hidden** somewhere in **Dorset**. Solve the clues at the beginning of the first three Winkton Abbey books to find the treasure…

To locate the prize you need persistence
And you may be wise to seek assistance
Six troublesome clues will take you there
And £1000 is yours to keep or share.

1. In a town in ancient Dorsetshire
   Begins our joyous game
   Before the *church*, and with some research
   Are the last three letters of Ameshin's name

   CHI

2. *Idol agent unlocks* the witches stolen soul
   Here is the first link towards your gold
   Look and see beneath where she sat
   This is where clue two is at
   A book of treasure is what you'll see
   Leading you to number three.

   Answer 1.
   Answer 2.

Winkton Abbey

WINKTON ABBEY

Book One

The Ghost's Answers

Jonathan Wedge

Winkton Abbey

Chapter One
The Shoe Incident

Lily could hardly breathe from so much walking; and she could hardly see. Drips of sweat kept leaking into her eyes, and her spectacles were slipping further towards the end of her nose. As such, the surrounding Dorset countryside had melted into a congealed blob of fuzzy objects.

Fiddling with a couple of emergency batteries in her pocket, Lily was impressed that her Walkman was still going. Her favourite album had been playing on repeat since they'd left the house, which seemed like days ago. The music was the only thing helping her legs struggle up the latest hill.

Blinking hard, Lily kept her eyes down on the road. Through blurred vision, her shoes looked like pixelated rectangles, as she imagined she was inside a computer game. She hoped that when she reached the top of the hill, she might uncover a hidden portal to another world; one that would whisk her far away from here. In reality, the best she could hope for, was that all this time, she had been walking in the opposite direction to where she was headed.

Quite fed up of not being able to see, Lily wiped her eyes using the sleeve of her jumper and pushed her glasses back to the top of her nose.

The fuzzy world disappeared, and the peak of the hill

came into focus. Her mother's hat was visible for a moment, before it dipped down the other side of the hill. Lily threw her head back in disbelief that more hills might lay beyond this one. A tunnel of trees hung above her head. She walked along, watching branches glide above her. Before reaching the top of the hill, she saw four faded white stripes of a zebra crossing. Lily thought this was strange, as there were no pavements here, only a pathway in and out of the forest on either side.

After seeing a zebra crossing, she began to question if she was getting close. She hoped she was, and she hoped she wasn't.

As long and arduous as this walk had been, Lily still wasn't certain she wanted to reach the end. There was a constant pain pulling at the inside of Lily's thighs. It hurt with every step. But the pain wasn't enough to stop her from worrying about spending her first night at boarding school. In fact, the long walk had only amplified her worries.

She'd not been able to stop thinking about what the children at her old school, Stakdale Junior, had told her. They had said that the school matrons at Winkton Abbey wouldn't care one bit if she wanted a hot chocolate before bed, or if she'd woken from a bad dream. Even a dream as horrifying as a giant wolf with drool dripping from its rabid teeth. The children said she'd be sent straight back to bed, without any word of concern. Indeed, the Stakdalers had made Lily believe that boarding school was as horrid as falling face first into a fresh cow-pat, every day, for the rest of your life. Whether or not they were correct, she would soon find out.

Lily saw her mother's hat come back into view. Over the last ten miles or so, Lily hadn't been able to fathom how her mother was managing to walk so fast, at the same time as carrying two suitcases filled with a term's worth of clothes. Lily had carried one case for all of ten minutes and even using two hands hadn't helped. She'd had no idea her mother was so strong, or that she was so weak.

Fed up, and dragging along behind, Lily wanted to ask what all children wanted to ask when they'd been on a long journey. But, before she could call out to ask how long was left until they arrived, she looked up. She adjusted her glasses once more, and from the top of the hill, she saw them—the gates of the school.

Tall, black, spiked, and firmly shut.

Lily removed her headphones and stopped. She wanted to turn and run. The school fence was just as tall, and just as spiked as the gates. It ran all the way around the visible perimeter of the school. Lily had never felt so intimidated.

Lily's mother put the suitcases down at the foot of one of the giant gate-pillars. Straightening up, she pressed the buzzer.

"Hello," a muffled voice blared out from the speaker on the wall.

"Um, hello there. This is Mrs Hannah Thicke. My

daughter, Lily Thicke, is starting here today. Can you open up the gates, please?"

Mrs Thicke waited for a reply. She waited a little longer; and having waited too long, she moved to press the buzzer once again. A voice shot out of the speaker. Her heart raced, making her pull her hand away, as if the button were somehow burning hot.

"We have no record of a *Lily Hanafick*. Did you not receive your gate-key in the post?" said the speaker.

Lily came up behind, grinning at the mix-up of their names. Poor Mrs Thicke was too exhausted, after walking so far, to find anything amusing. She stayed calm, nonetheless.

"Yes, we did receive it, dear, but that *key-thingy* is in one of our suitcases somewhere, and I thought it a lot easier to press a button and ask for the gate to be opened," she said.

"Always best to keep your gate-key in the car, so you can press the button when you approach..." the speaker said. "...the range is very good, I think you'll find," she added.

"We don't have a car," said Mrs Thicke.

"No car...? How did you get here?" the speaker said.

"We walked," said Mrs Thicke. "Would it be terribly too much trouble if you opened up the gate?"

"One can never be too careful? There are some strange goings on these days. Now, your name isn't on our system. Shall we start over...? Name please?" The speaker sounded almost too pleased at being such an efficient gate keeper.

Mrs Thicke was about ready to turn around and walk the fourteen miles back home, when Lily spotted a royal blue Rolls Royce rolling down the hill. The car moved in total silence. The engine was so smooth, all Lily heard, were the tyres gripping to the tarmac of the road. The driver tipped his cap to the two ladies, coming to a stop alongside them. Upon holding the gate-key up to the windscreen, the driver pressed the button, and the gates began to open.

Sitting in the back of this grand old motor car was a young boy, perhaps a year older than Lily. She presumed the man sitting beside him was his father. The boy looked far from happy, and when he caught Lily's eye, he scowled, wrinkling his nose up into a squashed sneer.

I wonder what his problem is? Lily thought to herself. *His father looks like a stern piece of work. Perhaps he hasn't had the easiest of upbringings.*

She chuckled inside, thinking how happy her feet would be, if she were the one sitting in the back of that car.

The electric gates couldn't have parted slowly enough for Lily. Once the iron spikes had jolted to a halt, that was it, a few more steps, and she was at her new school.

Heart pounding, Lily followed behind the Rolls Royce into the grounds of Winkton Abbey.

A flash of sunshine struck through Lily's glasses.

Squinting, she raised her arm to block the low September sun. The light was breaking through the trees of a not so distant hill. Once her eyes had readjusted, she saw her new school, in all of its English fineness.

The photographs Lily had seen from the prospectus hadn't given a true reflection of how green the playing fields really were, nor how perfectly maintained. A ride-on mower was presently motoring along, forming endless stripes of brilliant green across the sports fields. The smell of freshly cut grass danced up Lily's nose. Marked out with whiter-than-white lines, Lily had never seen hockey, rugby, and football pitches looking so pristine, and so flat and void of muddy patches. Over at the far side of the field, there was a cricket pavilion. And tea rooms, too. Lily thought the tea rooms alone might actually be bigger than her old school. Stakdale's grounds were no more than two portakabins and a small playground, with one broken swing.

Lily's wide eyes and understated smile gave Mrs Thicke the impression that Lily was thinking this place was incredible; indeed, she was thinking just that.

More school grounds lay beyond the playing fields. Lily saw a few small red flags flapping in the distance. It took her a moment to realise the flags belonged to the school's very own golf course. A golf course that weaved around the back of the manor house, a vast stone building, the towers of which stood guard at the head of the playing fields.

As grand as the manor house was, this was not what caught Lily's eye the most. She stared in awe at Winkton Abbey itself.

Not many schools have their own abbey, Lily thought.

Out of interest, Lily had spent some of the summer researching the history of Winkton Abbey, which she now knew dated back as far as 933AD. The church had a murky history, associated with powerful kings and treacherous monks. Made only more interesting, having been owned throughout its time by greedy earls and filthy-rich barons.

This is my new home, Lily thought.

Some kind of strange feeling trembled through her stomach. She had never seen a school as grand as this before. Stakdale Junior School, where she had been, from the age of five until the summer just gone, was a rundown, uncared for kind of place. The teachers didn't bother you if your uniform was scruffy from a fight, or whether you had done, or hadn't done any of your homework. It seemed Winkton Abbey couldn't be more different from the school-life Lily was used to.

Mrs Thicke was still admiring the look on Lily's face as she took it all in. "Don't worry about all of the riches you'll see here, Lily. Not having money does not make you worse than they are. Don't you let anyone tell you any different," she said.

"I've never met a rich person," said Lily. "Their cars are jolly nice."

She smiled, as her gaze followed the blue Rolls Royce down the winding driveway.

"Your father and I have saved our whole lives, ever since we moved to Dorset, so you can have the chance to have a car like that, one day," said Mrs Thicke.

"Maybe I could get some new shoes first," said Lily.

The blisters on her heels were awfully sore. Her new shoes were three sizes too big. And the fourteen mile walk to school, was not, as it turned out, *the best way to wear in your new shoes,* as Mr Thicke had told Lily, earlier that morning.

"We bought you those to grow into, dear," said Mrs Thicke, flashing a hopeful smile. "And I've just had a wonderful idea that I think will help."

Before Lily could question it, her mother had fished out a handful of tissues from her coat pocket and was busy stuffing them into Lily's shoes, behind her heels. This was only acceptable to Lily, because she was very aware of how much her parents had lived on baked beans on toast, and didn't drive a car, and didn't go on holidays, all so they could afford to send her to a good school. There was no way she could complain about ill-fitting shoes, or about having toilet tissue stuffed behind her heels, to help them fit better. After all, the tissues had eased the pain of the blisters.

Lily and her mother were soon nearing the main house. Car after car drove past them as they walked along the driveway. Lily watched in awe as Porsches, Range

Rovers, Mercedes and BMWs parked up in front of the main house. Over excited children jumped out of the cars, smiling wildly, greeting and hugging their friends.

Lily couldn't recall having ever had a friend that had hugged her after the holidays. A feeling of loneliness, and one of not knowing anyone here sent a monsoon of nerves flushing through her stomach. Walking towards a door, where the children were disappearing inside, she felt her throat grow tighter and increasingly dry with every step.

A man popped his head outside. "Hullo, do hurry up," he called over, stroking his beard, peering over the rim of his glasses. "I don't want to rush you, but you are the last to arrive, I believe."

Lily grabbed her mother by the arm, pulling her towards the door in a hurry, not wanting to be late.

"Erm, pupils only, please. Say goodbye out here, if you will. Suitcases and trunks over there," the teacher pointed to a stack of cases, before disappearing inside.

Lily looked up at her mother, she flung her arms around her waist, nestling a cheek hard into her stomach. The reality of not seeing her for six weeks, had only now crossed her mind. Even though, her parents had explained several times, that because of chapel on Sundays, school on Saturday mornings, and because of the long walk home, it made much more sense for Lily not to have any exeat weekends, but to stay in school until half-term arrived. All of a sudden, six weeks seemed like a very long time.

Lily let go of her mother's waist. "I know you and Dad told me everything will be okay here," she said. "And do you know what—I think you're right."

She smiled at her mother. Yet, somewhere inside she didn't know what she was doing. *I don't know anyone here...* she thought... *but, I can do this. Smile and walk inside,* she told herself. That was what she did. She kept smiling at her mother and waved goodbye.

It was time to go.

Time to grow up.

"Lily," her mother called out, a moment before she had reached the door.

Lily turned.

"Are you really okay?"

A part of Lily wanted to run back, take her mother's hand, never let go, and tell her she was terrified of walking through the door. The other part of her felt silly for all of the fuss she'd already made over the last few weeks about starting at a new school. Knowing that her mother had noticed she was only pretending to be okay, somehow made Lily feel okay.

"I'll be fine," said Lily.

This smile was genuine.

She stepped into the food hall, where the whole school seemed to be waiting for her. *Why couldn't I have turned up first, or in the middle? Why did I have to walk in last?* She thought.

Her smile grew wider as the wobble in her legs grew

wilder. She walked between the middle of two enormous bench-tables that stretched on and on and on.

The ceilings were high. The wooden floorboards creaked as she moved along. *If only those wooden beams could talk,* Lily thought.

She took great pleasure in noticing little details in a building, which others might have overlooked. What she noticed most of all about the food hall, were the paintings hanging on the walls. Aristocratic-looking, bearded old men, wearing ruffs, cloaks, and hats with little buckled-belts. The paintings sent a thrilling chill through Lily's body. Their pale, oil-painted eyes watched her as she moved along. *Don't look so scared*, she told herself, *everyone will think I'm nervous.* Which, of course, she was, and she was still sweating, which she hoped no one would notice.

She walked past the older boys and girls without too much bother. Then, as she carried on between the benches, she became all too aware that the younger years were watching her every step. The feeling was unbearable. Hundreds of eyes, including the eyes in the paintings, were all fixed upon her. Lily saw the boy from the Rolls Royce. She looked at him. This time he smiled. Except the smile was more of a smirk. He had noticed something rather odd. He had noticed a piece of toilet roll unravelling across the floor, behind Lily as she walked.

The boy stood up, clambering onto his chair, and he pointed at Lily.

"Look at her shoes!" he said, in delight. "There's toilet

17

roll stuffed into that girl's shoes!"

Lily looked down to see a white stream of toilet paper dragging along the floor, trailing out from her left shoe.

The entire school scrambled to their feet, squealing in delight to see the girl who had toilet roll stuffed down the back of her shoes. And once they'd seen it, they all pointed, and they all laughed. Even those boys and girls who would never laugh at someone else's misfortune, were laughing at the girl who had toilet roll stuffed in her shoes. It was such a silly thing for them to see.

Not for one moment would any of them have considered, why? Not for one moment would any of them have been able to figure out that Lily had walked fourteen miles to school that morning because she had no car; and in shoes that were three sizes too big because her parents couldn't afford new ones every time her feet grew; and because her mother had had the kind idea to ease the pain of her blisters by putting toilet roll down the back of her shoes.

Lily was petrified.

She stood on the spot, like a deer caught in wildfire with nowhere to run. She had no idea what she should do.

"SILENCE!" a woman shouted, appearing from nowhere, at the head of the benches.

The room felt as if all of the oxygen had been sucked out in an instant. Everyone sat down, sharply. All except Lily, who hadn't found a place to sit yet. And all except for the boy on the chair, who had instigated the laughs.

"YOU, BOY! Do *we* climb on the furniture at home?" the woman said.

"I don't think you've been to my house, miss. I don't see how *we* could have climbed on the furniture?" the boy said.

This was a stupid thing to say to Miss Warple. She was taller than most men. She had angry looking wrinkles set deep into her forehead, and the edges of her eyes squinted into a permanent scowl. A thinning of grey hairs covered her chin, and whenever she shouted, any living thing standing too close was caught in danger of being choked to death by the fumes of her hot, coffee-curdled breath.

"What is your name?" said Miss Warple.

"Robert Groom, miss," he said, hanging his head.

"You are new here, are you not?" said Miss Warple.

"First day, miss," said Robert.

"Well, *WE* do not climb on the furniture at Winkton Abbey. Is that clear?" said Miss Warple.

"Yes, miss," said Robert.

"Yes, Miss Warple," she said.

"Yes, Miss Warple," Robert repeated.

Lily couldn't help but enjoy Robert getting into trouble, and taking the attention away from her for a moment. She managed a smile.

"Good. I am the headmistress. I do deserve some respect. And you, girl, stop smiling, pick up your toilet roll, and sit. You're making the place look very untidy," said Miss Warple.

"Yes, Miss Warple. Except, I don't know what house I'm in just yet," said Lily.

"Name."

"It's Lily Thicke, miss."

The room giggled in delight at the surname.

"It's the thick-girl with a loo for a shoe," one boy called out.

The room laughed further.

"Who dares to call out?" Miss Warple snapped.

No one owned up. Miss Warple scoured the room for tell-tale signs. They all looked guilty to her.

"Lily Thicke, Tregonwell House. Hurry along," said Miss Warple, pointing over to a free seat.

Lily gladly gathered the toilet roll and sat down. Thanks to Robert Groom, her entrance to the school had been a nightmare.

She took a seat next to a pretty blonde girl. Lily herself was not unpretty, but she kept her hair short because it was easier for her mother to trim; and because of her good reading habit she wore a pair of thin rimmed spectacles. Both features took a little something away from the natural beauty she did possess. The blonde girl with curly hair smiled at her. Lily managed a shy look in return.

Miss Warple slapped a hand hard on the bench top. Anyone who hadn't been looking her way, was now.

"Let me welcome you to the new school year," said

Miss Warple. "This autumn term is different to previous years. This is the first time we have allowed a younger stream of pupils into the school. We believe that attending the same school from a young boy or girl, until you are a young man or woman is essential, if all of you Winktonians are to go on and achieve greater things in this world," Miss Warple paused to stare at the children closest to her. "Stand up. Look sharp, new little ones," she said.

Lily shot up first.

The other smaller children began to stand up around her. There were some children she instantly hoped that she would make friends with. There was the pretty blonde girl who was now standing up beside her; there was a stiff looking boy with curly hair who seemed to smile a lot; he was probably just as nervous as Lily was. And three seats away there was also a kind looking Japanese girl, who Lily had noticed was in the middle of reading a book on famous crimes in Dorset.

Lily didn't always go by how people looked, but you do sometimes know by the look of someone if you're going to get along with them or not. Out of the thirty or so children standing, these three were who she thought she would get on with the best.

Miss Warple continued, "You new ones are a mixture of lower and upper third forms—"

The bearded teacher, who had spoken to Lily outside, tapped Miss Warple on the shoulder and whispered a few words in her ear.

"Hmm, not so much of a mixture, it would seem. There is only one girl here who is at lower third age, but her August birthdate qualifies her for both years. Lily Thicke you are now in the upper third form. Lucky you, in the last five seconds you have skipped a whole year of school, and you are the youngest pupil ever to attend Winkton Abbey. Everyone, please help her whenever she needs it," said Miss Warple.

Lily shrank inside. She had no idea she was going to be the youngest pupil at the school. With her birthday in August, she'd always been the oldest in the class.

No one will want to be friends with the youngest girl in the school, she thought. *Especially one who's made such a fool of herself on the first day.*

The blonde girl nudged her, leaning in to whisper whilst Miss Warple carried on talking. "Don't worry, Lily. Tregonwell House takes care of its own," she said. "My older sister has been here for two years, and she told me never to worry. If you get plenty of house credits, you'll be just fine. I'm Izzy by the way."

"Thanks, Izzy, that's good to know," Lily whispered back. "It might not be much fun being the youngest in the school. What are house credits?" she said.

"The four houses of the school compete every year for the Winkton Abbey Cup. Being good at sports and playing in the school teams is usually the best way to win house credits. Drake House won the WAC last year. Not this year though. Not if I've got anything to do with it. Are you any good at hockey or netball? Those are my favourites," said Izzy.

Lily didn't know what to say. "I'm okay at hockey, I guess."

Lily never was good at lying. She didn't know why she couldn't have told Izzy that sports really weren't her thing, but she didn't want to make herself seem even more useless than she already had.

"… and that concludes my welcome to the new school year," said Miss Warple.

Lily hadn't been listening for the last minute or so, and after talking to Izzy, she was even more worried that she wouldn't fit in at her new school.

Miss Warple kept talking. "Lessons start at 9am sharp, tomorrow morning. You will find your new term timetables on your pillows in your dormitories. I trust this school year will go as well as we all want it to," she said, before turning and marching out of the food hall, without another word.

A light breeze of oxygen seemingly returned to the room. Now everyone could breathe again, the mood lightened with laughter and chatter filling the food hall.

An older looking version of Izzy came bounding over. "Hey Izz, you're in our dorm now. We did have Lily Thicke, but the girls voted her out," she said.

"Oh, okay. Thanks, Emi," said Izzy, trying not to sound too happy. She sent an awkward smile Lily's way

23

as Emi bounced off, back towards her friends.

Lily shrugged her shoulders. "Don't worry about it, Izzy. You should board with your sister anyway," she said.

"I hope you get a good dorm. It really does make all the difference. I boarded at Homewood School for the first-time last year, and I reckon you're going to love it," said Izzy.

Lily wasn't so sure about that. She'd never been away from her parents for longer than a school day before. Now she wouldn't see them for weeks.

"Oi, Loo-Shoe," a dark haired, older girl said.

The insulting new nickname could only be meant for one person. Lily turned to face the girl. "Hello," she said, accepting the nickname without a fuss.

"You're in dorm twenty-four, with us," the girl said. She pointed over to the Japanese girl. "*Fortune Cookie*, that goes for you too. Grab your suitcases and get upstairs. We've got your initiation to get on with," she said, strutting off with two other girls following behind.

Did she just call the Japanese girl, Fortune Cookie? Lily couldn't believe it. She wanted to say something and stick up for the girl.

"I know what you're thinking," the girl said. "Don't get yourself into trouble on my account."

"She can't get away with that," said Lily.

"She called you *Loo-Shoe*, isn't that just as bad?"

"Not quite, no. If you don't want me to mention it

though, then I won't," said Lily.

"The funny thing is, fortune cookies are supposed to be Chinese. My dad is Japanese, and my mum is Canadian. Funnier still, the fortune cookie was invented in America. So, it really was a stupid insult," the girl said.

Lily blew a laugh out of her nose. With all that had been going on, and with her day going so terribly badly, she didn't think anyone could make her laugh, but this girl had managed to.

Lily was filled with instant warmth to have met someone who could degrade an insult into being nothing more than nonsense; someone who was not only going to be in her dorm, but the same House too.

The girl stuck out a hand. "My name is Ameshin Chi," she said.

Lily had never shaken hands before. She thought she did well for her first time. "Good to meet you, Ameshin. I'm Lily Thicke."

"I think everyone knows who you are," said Ameshin.

Chapter Two
Ghost-Board

Lily and Ameshin stood staring at the number twenty-four stuck on to the door of their dormitory.

The Winkton Abbey crest was finely carved into the door, and the motto, "*Non deficere, et Vincere.*" was painted in gold below the crest.

"Never give up, and you win," said Ameshin.

"You can read Latin?" said Lily, knowing some girls their age who could hardly read English.

"It helps to know languages that no one else does, just so at times like this, you can feel really smart," said Ameshin.

Lily *was* impressed. "Shall we go in?" she said.

"It might be a better option to sleep out here," said Ameshin.

Lily agreed, but nudged the door open, nonetheless. The room was dark. Silent. They couldn't see a thing beyond the dying rays of dim hall-light which lit up a small portion of wooden flooring.

Lily went inside first, feeling along the wall for a light-switch. Ameshin came in after her and the door slammed shut behind them.

Pressing her palms in different places along the wall, Lily couldn't manage to find the light switch.

"Hello?" she said to the black room.

Screams pierced through the dark. A ball of fire tore through the air towards Lily. Eyes, mouths, and faces lit up in flames all around the room. Girls were screaming with shrill cries. Lily and Ameshin screamed much louder than the other girls. The lights came on. Ameshin didn't stop screaming.

The girl with the long dark hair from the food hall was holding a deodorant can in one hand and a lighter in the other. She lit a flame and sprayed the deodorant, sending a stream of fire into the air. "All right, it was only a joke," she said.

Ameshin calmed herself down.

"Jinny, you do take it too far sometimes," one of the other girls said. "Miss Warple told us to look after the young ones, not terrify them."

"I'm only having a laugh, Claire. They know that— don't you girls?" said Jinny.

A fake smile hid the fright pounding inside of Lily. "Oh sure, I mean, it's not like we thought there was a dragon in our dorm or something. Right, Ameshin?" she said.

"Maybe I did, but that's probably because there are a lot of dragons where I come from," said Ameshin.

"Really?" said Jinny.

The other girls laughed.

"Oh shut-up, you lot. You know I'm gullible," Jinny said. "And don't you be so smart with your mouth, little one. A sharp tongue can get you into a lot of trouble."

"It can get you *out* of a lot of trouble, too," said Ameshin.

Despite Jinny's angry face, Lily and the other girls let out a variance of laughter. It promptly stopped when Jinny turned to look at her friends.

Looking back to the new girls, she said, "So, you're a lippy-beggar are you? Let's get on with this initiation. I bet you won't be so clever then. Maybe we'll hear that scream again." Jinny pressed into Ameshin's shoulder with a firm finger. "Laura, lock the door."

As commanded, Laura slid the bolt, and Lily and Ameshin were now locked in the dorm with their new roommates, Jinny, Claire, and Laura.

It looked to Lily like Jinny was the alpha-female of the dorm. Everyone did as she said, and why wouldn't they? Lily certainly wouldn't want to go up against her, she didn't seem the type to show any mercy. Especially to younger ones. A classic bully. Claire seemed a little kinder, the type who just goes along with it for an easy life. And Laura didn't look so bad; she was tall, a bit boyish looking, and tubby, but she had a nice smile, which she revealed once she'd closed the door.

"Okay, let's get the board out," said Laura.

Diving under the bed she pulled out a wooden board and placed it on the floor. Written across the board were numbers from one to ten, and the letters of the alphabet. The girls got on their knees, forming a circle around the board.

"Have either of you ever seen a board like this before?" said Jinny.

Ameshin and Lily shook their heads.

"This is a ghost-board," said Jinny, lighting some tea lights in glass candle holders, and placing them down. "Claire, turn out the lights, will you."

Claire hopped up and flicked the switch, hurrying back to the game. The girls were now sitting around the ghost-board. Five faces flickering in the candlelight.

"What, exactly, does a ghost-board do?" Lily asked.

"It communicates to the ghosts in the school," said Jinny.

As much as Lily was going to enjoy sharing a room with Ameshin, right at that moment she wished that Izzy had been in this dorm instead of her, as she was supposed to be. Lily would rather have taken her chances in the dorm with the pretty girls. She'd bet anything they weren't playing games with ghost-boards right now.

"The game is really simple, all you have to do is ask a question," said Claire.

"Don't worry, it's such good fun. I'll go first," said Laura. She thought for a moment. "Will I get kissed by a boy this year?" she said.

Lily couldn't believe her eyes. One of the glass candle holders slid across the board, without being touched. She hadn't seen anyone move. The candle was sliding by itself.

She figured this house was a strange old place as soon

as she'd stepped inside. She accepted that some oddities were to be expected in a house with hundreds of years of history behind it—but ghosts? *What other mysteries does this place hold?* She wondered.

The candle stopped beneath the *Y*, and it moved across to *E*, and stopped on *S*.

Laura cooed to herself, presumably picturing who she hoped the boy would be that she would kiss.

"Can I ask a question next?" said Ameshin.

Jinny held out a finger, stopping her before she said another word. "The only rule is, you can ask just one question at the beginning of the year. There have been too many stories about when the game has gone wrong, and people have been hurt. But, it's too much fun to stop playing altogether," she said.

"Okay," said Ameshin. "I'd like to know—" She paused to think of a question. "—what book will we be studying in English this term?"

Jinny groaned. "Ahh, that's boring," she said.

Regardless of the groaning, the candle began to move. R-O-M-E-O-A-N-D-J-U-L-I-E-T the candle spelt out. Ameshin was happy with that answer, if by some pure fluke the ghost had answered correctly. She really didn't see how a ghost who had haunted an old house for a few hundred years might know what the upper third English curriculum would be for this year. That's if there even was such a thing as ghosts, which she very much doubted.

"Will everyone in this room be at Winkton Abbey until

they are sixteen?" is what Claire asked next.

N-O. The ghost replied.

They all wondered who from among them would be there, and who wouldn't. Even Ameshin thought the same, regardless of not believing in ghosts.

"Will anyone be expelled this year?" said Jinny.

Y-E-S. The ghost spelt out.

The girls couldn't help but be excited by the answer. Questions burst through their minds. *Why would someone get expelled? Who would it be? When would it happen?*

There was only one more turn remaining, and it belonged to Lily. The girls' candlelit faces stared at her. Tiny flames flickered away in her eyes as she thought about what she could ask out of all the questions she could ask.

"I'd like to save my question, if I may?" said Lily.

"Until when?" said Jinny.

"Until such a time that I have a question worth asking," said Lily.

"I don't mind," said Laura.

"I don't mind either," said Claire.

"Very well, Lily, save your question, if it suits you. Remember, we must all be present when you ask it," said Jinny. She smiled. "I'm glad you two aren't scared of ghosts or anything. It's just a bit of fun, just like everything is really."

"I never knew such a thing existed," said Lily.

"That's what you've come to Winkton Abbey for, Lily,

to learn new things," said Laura.

The ghost-board was cleared away, and after Lily and Ameshin, and the rest of the girls had unpacked their suitcases, they flicked through their timetables which they found on their pillows, and they settled down for a long night's sleep.

Lily and Ameshin were each on the bottom bunks, and their beds were positioned just close enough for future whispers in the dark. Claire and Laura were on the top bunks, and Jinny had a bed all to herself, tucked into a bay window.

The lights went out at 20:30, and Lily thought about what she might learn at her new school. She had already learnt that some boys are cruel, even if they have rich fathers; some girls, *like Jinny*, like to make fun of people and not take life too seriously; and she'd seen that that ghosts are frightfully clever things, knowing the answers to all sorts of questions, but perhaps not as clever as her new friend, Ameshin.

Lily thought about what question she would ask the school ghosts, and she wondered what further strangeness might appear from the cracks of this old place. Before she fell asleep, one final thought struck — she needn't have worried so much on her long walk to school that morning, Winkton Abbey school was a million times better than Stakdale Junior.

Chapter Three

A Disappearing Act

At lunchtime on a wet and windy Wednesday, something had seemingly upset all of the teachers. A quarrelling rabble was forming in the staff room. Their rants and hisses made a noise like that of a swarm of upset bees.

They were all cursing and complaining about Lily.

Within the first few days of term, the teachers had been finding out that when it came to learning, Lily was the most curious of girls. This behaviour stemmed from one tiny thing, her surname, Thicke.

After years of name calling, Lily was determined to never be called 'thick' by anyone again. To this end she questioned most things, and never accepted anything, until she was sure that the facts of the matter were correct. And the more she thought about things, the more she thought there had to be a reason for everything. And, of course, she was right. There is a reason why people put on carefully selected clothes every morning; there is a reason why hair grows on every part of every body; there is a reason why the sky is blue; there is a reason why bananas are yellow; there is even a reason why wasps exist, even though they seem to buzz about for no other reason than to annoy people. There is a reason for everything. Except, we don't think about all of those reasons, because if we did, it would drive us mad.

We, as humans, simply like to *just accept* that things simply are the way they are. Not Lily. She didn't ever *just accept* anything.

Unfortunately, though, she didn't realise that asking questions all of the time was annoying. She had behaved like this for so long now that she found it quite normal to be inquisitive.

Her old teachers at Stakdale never had the time to answer Lily's questions, but here with such small class sizes at Winkton Abbey, she was sure the teachers would help her learn everything she'd ever wanted to know. After all, she expected that everyone else wanted to know everything, too. Well, not that Lily would have believed it, but most people are quite happy not knowing why it rains acid on Venus, or why a butterfly's taste-buds are on its feet, or even why turtles breathe out of their bottoms.

By only the third day of term it was the questions which she was asking that was driving her teachers mad.

Mr Ballard, the English teacher, had a rant going with the R.E teacher, Miss Hare. And Mr Tate, the bearded history teacher, was chewing the ear off of Mr Potts, the school librarian, who wasn't paying much attention. He really didn't care much for noise—or much for conversation for that matter. Mr Potts rather liked Lily. He'd duly noted that if she was learning then she was being quiet, and during evening prep when she was sitting in Mr Potts' library, she was reading and learning, and being nice and quiet.

"HUSH, HUSH," a shrill voice called above the rabble.

Miss Warple walked into the middle of the chaotic room. She disliked chaos, and her staff knew it. The noise died to a whimper.

"It appears we have a new brat in tow. A brat that is causing you all to behave like wet, moaning mops. Now, tell me, what is the worst of Lily Thicke, and I shall deal with her," she said.

Mr Tate raised his hand. "She asked me which country had had the most soldiers killed in the great-war. I told her it was Russia, and then she asked me how many deaths there were to the closest million, and if I was sure that I knew which war the great-war was, and whether I was one hundred percent on my answer. It was terrifying," he said.

Mrs Grand, the geography teacher, stood up. "She asked me to give her a list of every official country in the world, and to write down the capital city of each one, and give the native languages they speak. That would take me until Christmas, Miss Warple," she said, while pulling at a strand of curled, silver hair.

The room burst back into a buzz of annoyance.

"SILENCE!" shouted Miss Warple. "So, what you're telling me is that this brat is here to learn?"

"Yes," answered Mr Tate, and Mrs Grand, and the rest of the room all at once.

Laughter filled the air. A laugh none of the staff had heard before now. It was a squeak and a choke, mixed with a piggish grunt, and it continued for an uncomfortable amount of time.

Miss Warple's contorted face straightened out with a twitch, and her usual serious poise returned.

"I will not discourage learning in my school. If a pupil asks a question and is quashed for it, what does that make us?" said Miss Warple.

No one responded.

"Bad teachers. And are we bad teachers?" Miss Warple asked, looking down on all who stood beneath her manly frame.

"No, Miss Warple," the teachers replied.

"Good. You will deal with the questions from Ms Thicke as well as you can, and if that isn't at all well, we shall have some staff reviews. You all know that jobs can oh-so-easily become available, just like that!" She clicked her fingers. "Now, I should like to meet the new brat properly and see how she is getting on. What is her next lesson?"

"Double PE with me, Miss Warple," said Mrs Williams.

Miss Warple began to walk towards the door. "Very good, Williams. I trust she can't ask too many questions when she's running about, can she? Send her to my office before prep."

With that, Miss Warple slammed the door behind her.

*

Lily and Ameshin were in the food hall, finishing the last spoonful of their lunch. Mrs Plumley, the school dinner lady, had fed them a glorious sausage casserole, and chocolate pudding with chocolate custard for dessert.

A teacher, who neither of them knew, leant across from the end of the bench. "Is your name Ameshin?" he asked.

"Yes, sir," said Ameshin. "How did you know that?"

"Your father requested a phone call with me not so long ago to explain how, *his little girl*, needed special attention with her violin tutorage. He told me quite a lot about you. Whenever you need my help, do come and find me in room 5b. My name is on the door, *Mr Taplow*. I'm your music teacher," he said.

"Thank you, Mr Taplow. I could really do with somewhere to practice. Is the music room free during break-times?" said Ameshin.

"Of course, it would be a pleasure to hear you play. You're lucky to have such a violin as yours. I have always wanted one of those," said Mr Taplow, admiring Ameshin's violin case.

Ameshin thanked Mr Taplow and the girls went on their way to begin an afternoon of PE. They were still getting used to the labyrinthine corridors at the school, but at least by now they'd managed to remember where the lockers were, which was where they were heading.

"Will you have to practice violin every break-time?" said Lily.

Ameshin could tell Lily was worried about losing her only friend for large parts of the day.

"I need to be ready for the Christmas concert at the end of term. You'll be all right, Lily. Why don't you find something interesting to do while I'm practising?" said Ameshin.

"I'll have to do something," said Lily. She gave it a thought for a second, before remembering she had to ask a more pressing question. "What did Mr Taplow mean about having a violin *like yours*?" Lily asked.

Ameshin stopped in the middle of the hallway and placed her violin case on top of an old cabinet, thinking it was better to show Lily than to explain. She flipped open the violin case.

"My violin's an antique. It was carved by one of the finest makers in Japan, Machiko Murata," said Ameshin. "It's over one-hundred-and-fifty years old."

"Hey, she's a beauty," a voice said from behind the girls. "How well do you play?"

When Ameshin and Lily turned around, they saw the head boy, with several of his fifth former friends. Some admired the violin. The double-M mark carved on the side would have meant nothing to them, but it was a fine-looking instrument, even to the untrained eye.

Lily and Ameshin knew who the head boy was, not least of all because instead of wearing a blue blazer, like the other boys, he wore a smart brown-tweed blazer that complemented the blue and gold of the Winkton Abbey school tie.

"I've been grade eight since I was seven," said Ameshin, sounding a little shy. She didn't speak to boys much, and especially not to older boys.

"That's impressive. I'm only grade seven. Maybe you can teach me a thing or two," the head boy said.

"It's just about practicing hard really, but if you'd like to practice together then I would like that," said Ameshin.

"Come on, Tom, let's leave the little girls to it," one of the other boys said, walking onwards.

"Wait up, guys," said Tom. "You don't think I want to practice with a little girl, do you?" The head boy ran off after his friends, without another word to Ameshin.

Ameshin closed the violin case and pulled the leather straps in through the buckles. They started off again to their lockers.

"Boys are idiots, aren't they?" said Lily.

"I suppose. I don't like practicing with other people anyway. I was only being polite," said Ameshin.

"It really is a beautiful violin though," said Lily.

"My father looked after it very well, and my grandfather always said that this violin is the pride of our family. Five generations of the Chi family have played it in the Japanese Symphony Orchestra, and I must follow suit," said Ameshin, with a determined smile.

"Wow, my family can hardly play a CD," said Lily.

Ameshin chuckled heartily, unlocking the padlock to her locker. She then unlocked the locker itself and took out her sports bag, carefully placing her violin inside. She locked up the locker, and clicked back the padlock, tugging down on it to make sure it was secure.

Lily, on the other hand, leant in awkwardly close to her locker, and unlocked her padlock with a key that was attached to a necklace.

"That's a clever idea," said Ameshin.

"I'm always losing my keys. This way I never can," said Lily.

She grabbed her sports bag and slammed her locker door shut. She nearly screamed when the face of an old man appeared right behind where her locker door had been.

Lily hadn't seen or heard him coming.

"Sorry to scare you, there," the man said. He grinned, revealing gaps holes in his mouth where a couple of teeth were missing.

Lily smiled back. She would still rather have screamed. There was something off about this man. It was the way he moved without hardly making a sound. He was dressed all in black, which made him almost invisible in the dark corridor, but for a head sitting on his shoulders.

"Don't mind me. People hardly ever notice me. I'll keep on sweeping, if you don't mind," the man said.

At that point, Lily and Ameshin realised he was cleaning the corridor. He hadn't just been bending down to hide behind lockers and scare them. He was the school caretaker, going about his business.

"Good day, sir," said Lily, and off they hurried, both dreading an afternoon of PE.

Out on the sports field, Mrs Williams told the upper third class to run around the entire field three times. As soon as the task was issued, Izzy, and the sportier ones shot off at once. Robert bumped into Lily on his way past.

"Hey, *Robert Groom.* I'll report you if you carry on like this," Lily shouted.

Robert kept running, as if he hadn't heard.

"Ignore him, Lily. Come on, let's get on with it," said Ameshin.

"Do I always have to ignore people in the wrong?" said Lily.

Ameshin didn't answer, she began to jog on. Lily stayed put.

"I'll catch up with you in a minute. I've got some questions to ask Mrs Williams," said Lily.

Miss Warple had been wrong, Lily did have plenty of questions to ask. She asked about what muscle groups would benefit from running three times around the field, and how many calories that would burn, and what was the best food to eat to recover the lost calories from such a long run.

"Lily Thicke, please just run, and you can eat what you like, just not too much of it," Mrs Williams told her.

Lily sensed the fed-up tone in her teacher's voice and ran on to catch up with Ameshin at the back of the group.

Mrs Williams shouted after her. "Lily, Miss Warple wants to see you in her office before prep tonight. Don't you dare forget," she said.

How could I forget something like that? Lily thought, as she hurried along. *I wonder what that's about?*

Lily caught up to Ameshin.

"What did you think about English today?" said Lily, doing her best to look like she knew how to run.

"I like Mr Ballard. He's firm, and he doesn't mind having a shout, which keeps John Porter, that class clown from disrupting everyone," said Ameshin.

"I was thinking more of what you thought about Romeo and Juliet being given as this terms study book. Like the ghost told you it would," said Lily.

"The dorm girls were pulling your leg, Lily. That game isn't real. It's far beyond any scientific explanation, and that means it can't be true," said Ameshin.

"I don't know. I have a strange feeling about this place. It's just so old and creepy," said Lily.

"Well, nothing has happened yet to show *me* that anything strange is going on here. I'm sorry, I don't believe in ghosts," said Ameshin.

"I know what is strange, and that's me having to go and see Miss Warple before prep. Will you come along and stand outside? In case you hear me screaming from being tortured or something," said Lily.

Ameshin cackled.

"I'm serious," said Lily.

"I know you are," said Ameshin.

Lily's breath was running out. She stopped to rest her legs, which were still aching from her walk to school. Ameshin kept going. "Don't stop, Lily. It's always so much harder to get going again," she said.

Lily stumbled on with her run. "Yes, tell me, why is that the case?" she said.

Ameshin ignored the question and ran on.

Mrs Williams made Lily and Ameshin complete the three laps, even though it took them fifteen minutes longer than everyone else.

"We are going to have to work on your fitness levels, aren't we girls. You won't get any credits towards the Winkton Abbey Cup if you carry on like this," Mrs Williams said.

Normally, Lily didn't mind being told that she'd have to do something, but Mrs Williams was a little bit rotund herself, and Lily would like to see how quickly *she* could run around the sports field three times.

"Can you show us the pace next time please, Mrs Williams?" said Lily.

Mrs Williams changed the subject. "Run along and shower, and don't be late to see Miss Warple," she said.

Lily displayed a look of smugness as they hobbled off to the showers. She didn't think Mrs Williams would be pushing her too hard during PE in the future, now that she knew Lily might try and get her to join in with them.

After showering, the girls' cheeks were glowing red. And somehow, even having run so far, they were full of energy as they bounced along an empty corridor towards their lockers.

"I'd better hurry, I'm running late to see Miss Warple. Are you coming with me?" said Lily, bending over to open her locker.

"I'd better go to prep. Good luck though. I'll see you at dinner, shall I?" said Ameshin.

At that moment, Ameshin both froze and threw herself away from her locker, at the same time as letting out a scream that caused Lily to nearly strangle herself with the key chain around her neck.

Ameshin's back slammed into the wall. Lily had no doubt she would have thrown herself back further and fallen to the floor, had the wall not been there.

"What's the matter?" said Lily.

Ameshin dropped to her knees, sobbing. She hid her face behind her hands.

Lily looked down at her friend, clueless as to what had her so frantic, knowing that Ameshin wasn't the type to get so upset so quickly.

After several questions, Lily couldn't get a word out of Ameshin. She couldn't figure it out. Then she turned her attention to the inside of Ameshin's locker.

It was empty.

Her violin was gone.

"Where is your violin?" said Lily.

"My father is going to kill me," said Ameshin, sobbing.

"It's impossible. You have the keys to the padlock, and the locker. I saw you lock them both up," said Lily.

"Where is it…? I want to go home," said Ameshin.

Lily helped Ameshin to her feet. "Come on, Amie, don't let this get you down. The good thing about something that's missing is that it still exists somewhere, and can always be found," said Lily. "It's not like it's been destroyed in a fire."

"You think we can find it?" said Ameshin, looking brighter.

"A mystery like this deserves to be solved," said Lily.

She offered a tissue, Ameshin took it, drying her eyes. "Where would we start?" she said.

"It couldn't be Thomas Allen, the head boy, could it?" said Lily.

"He seemed nice enough, I couldn't imagine so," said Ameshin.

"One of his friend's maybe? Who else saw you with the violin today?" asked Lily.

"Everyone. I've carried it with me all morning," said Ameshin.

"It's a shame *he* can't tell us," said Lily, looking up at a portrait of a man on the wall.

One of the frightful paintings seemed to hang on every wall in the school. The golden badge below the painting said, "Joseph Edison 1752". The man in the painting was grey-haired, high-browed, dressed in fine clothes, holding a tricorne-hat under one arm. The oil strokes made him look mysterious and ghostly.

The girls looked at each other after being struck by the same thought. "The ghost-board!" they said.

Within one minute of the idea striking and having run much faster than they had in PE, the two of them were in their dorm with the curtains drawn, lights off, candles lit, and legs crossed, sitting at the ghost-board.

"Are you ready?" said Lily.

"Ready," Ameshin replied.

Lily took a deep breath and asked the ghost-board her question. "Who took Ameshin's violin out of the locker today?" she said.

The candle began to move quickly between the letters. The girls had to concentrate hard to keep up with the answer.

U-S-E—Y-O-U-R—E-Y-E-S—
Y-O-U—W-I-L-L—S-E-E—
S-O-M-E-O-N-E—H-E-R-E—
W-H-O—S-H-O-U-L-D—N-O-T—B-E

"What does that mean? That doesn't answer the question," said Lily. "Tell us who it was, you silly ghost!"

"Someone is here who shouldn't be here," said Ameshin, thinking hard. "Who would that be?"

When the door opened, their frustrations turned to panic.

Before the ghost-board could be hidden, the lights came on and the door was shut.

"This isn't any good. This isn't any good at all," said Jinny, standing over the girls. She threw a bag onto her bed and stepped closer.

"No one plays this game without my permission," Jinny said, through gritted teeth. She grabbed Lily by the ear, pulling her off her feet.

"Hey, let go of her," Ameshin shouted, lunging to help her friend.

Jinny swatted her away with ease.

"You two need to learn a few lessons in respect," said Jinny, twisting Lily's ear harder.

"If you'll just listen to what I have to say—" said Lily.

"No, you listen to what *I* have to say. If I catch either of you with that board out again, it'll be more than your ear that gets it. Do you hear?" said Jinny.

"Yes, Jinny," said Lily.

"And you?" Jinny said to Ameshin.

Ameshin nodded, looking terrified.

The door opened, and as quick as a cat, Jinny dropped Lily's ear, even before she saw it was the head boy.

"What's all the noise in here?" said Tom Allen.

"Hi, Tom," said Jinny, flirting with a smile.

"Jinny, what's going on?" he said.

"The girls are playing forbidden games, but I can handle it. There's no need to punish them," said Jinny.

"No candles in the dorms. Come on, girls, don't be stupid. And why aren't you all in prep anyway?" said Tom.

All three of them started blurting out excuses.

"Okay," Tom said, raising his voice. "I don't want excuses. Make your way down for the last twenty minutes, and then it's dinnertime."

Lily couldn't do any work during Prep, and she wasn't interested in eating dinner afterwards. What she did do was watch everyone as they were doing their homework, and watch them all as they were eating their dinner. While she watched them, she was trying to figure out who might have taken the violin.

She soon realised it could have been anyone. She couldn't rule out any of the teachers either.

Lily knew that someone here in this room had done something awful to her friend, and with the help of the ghost's answer, she was going to find them.

Chapter Four
The Stare

As soon as Thursday morning assembly began, the first assembly of Lily's school career, a queer feeling rumbled through her stomach. Miss Warple was standing at a lectern, watching pupils file into place onto the church pews. Everyone remained standing, Lily presumed they were not allowed to sit until asked to do so.

The younger pupils were at the front, and the older you were, the further back your seat was situated from the teachers. This arrangement meant Lily and Ameshin were presently standing no more than a few metres away from where Miss Warple was gripping her long fingers around the edges of the lectern.

Not that Lily or Ameshin knew it yet, but Miss Warple generally used this time of week as an opportunity to impress her high standards on to young, impressionable minds. She also used the assembly to put anyone straight who had not been keeping in line with how she wanted her pupils to behave. The rumble in Lily's stomach grew stronger. She was sure she wasn't hungry, she'd had two poached eggs for breakfast.

"Sit!" Miss Warple said, looking even more irritable than normal.

Everyone sat.

Having noticed the Head's tight grip on the lectern and with a feeling that something was wrong, it then occurred to Lily, that during PE yesterday, Mrs Williams had told her, *twice*, to go and see the Headmistress in her office before prep.

Heat rose up under the collar of her blouse. Lily could not quite believe that she had skipped an appointment with Miss Warple. The high stone walls of the abbey seemingly shifted higher, whilst the ceilings pressed down onto her. She was trapped. Her breath was gone. She felt as if everyone was staring and laughing at her, again.

One thing, however, that was not in her imagination, was that Miss Warple looked utterly furious, and she was staring at Lily like a woman possessed. Her eyes were not blinking. She did not look anywhere else but straight into Lily's eyes.

"We shall begin by singing the hymn. Stand," Miss Warple directed.

The organ pipes charged up an F-chord, and the school assembly stood up, five seconds after they'd been told to sit, to sing the morning hymn, *Morning Has Broken*.

Miss Warple as good as screeched every word at the top of her voice, and never once did she take her eyes away from staring at Lily. Lily felt quite poorly by the end of the song. On the verge of fainting, she was, but at least she knew she had a good excuse for not making it to the Head's office the previous evening.

The hymn was soon over, and Miss Warple went on to talk about how well the new pupils were fitting in, and that trials for hockey, netball, football, and rugby would begin next week. And every subject that was broached gave Lily hope that she was imagining the stare. Except, she wasn't. The whole time Miss Warple spoke, she kept her eyes fixed on Lily, and the school was becoming quite aware of the stare.

Pupils tapped each other on the shoulder, pointing it out to those who had missed the blindingly obvious fact, that Warple was staring at one of the upper thirds. Those closest to the front could see the upper third in question was Lily Thicke.

"Next week," said Miss Warple, adjusting her body to lean on the lectern, gaining an inch closer to Lily, "we shall begin weekly updates for the Winkton Abbey Cup. The score, as it stands, is all-square. No-one has a earnt a credit in the first days of term. However, there is one misdemeanour."

The hall was so quiet you could hear the blinking of curious eyes looking about the place, and the whispered sounds of excitement as to what was coming.

"Lily Thicke, stand up," said Miss Warple.

Lily shot up from her seat faster than a frog's tongue flicks through the air to catch a fly.

"One discredit to Tregonwell House," said Miss Warple.

Everyone in Lily's house groaned.

"But, miss, I—"

"Don't you dare talk back to *me*," said Miss Warple.

Lily shrunk into a hole. She knew she shouldn't talk back to teachers, but she had a perfectly good excuse. If she was only allowed to explain.

"Were you, or were you not, told to meet me in my office before prep yesterday evening?" said Miss Warple.

"I was," said Lily, talking down to her feet.

"Straighten yourself up, girl. We keep our appointments in this school. I am also well informed you were not present in prep, either. I can't imagine what else was so important that it kept you from being where you were supposed to be, two times over," said Miss Warple.

"Sorry, Miss Warple. It won't happen again." said Lily.

"Sit down, Ms Thicke—I don't want you to be the only one standing every time the school is gathered in the same room. This is the second time in five days. You will get yourself a bad reputation," said Miss Warple.

Lily sat down without another word.

Ameshin stood up, raising her hand.

Miss Warple adjusted her glasses, checking to make sure her eyes were seeing things correctly. Lily pulled at Ameshin's blazer, trying to get her to sit back down, but Ameshin was acting as if the Headmistress didn't faze her one bit.

"If you're going to stick up for your friend, you can have another discredit for the house," said Miss Warple.

"No, miss, I need to tell you something," said Ameshin.

"Well, what is it?" Miss Warple said.

"My violin, an antique violin, which is insured for a lot of money, was taken from my locker yesterday, and I would like it returned," said Ameshin, speaking up, so the whole school could hear.

"Are you suggesting the item was stolen?" said Miss Warple. "Because things are never *stolen* at this school, my dear. I assure you of that."

"My locker was double locked with my violin inside, and after PE, my violin was gone. Make of that what you will, Miss Warple," said Ameshin.

"It must be a mistake. You have placed it somewhere and forgotten. It will turn up. These things always do," said Miss Warple.

"It was no mistake, Miss Warple. A violin, double locked inside a locker, cannot simply disappear —"

"Sit down," said Miss Warple. "That is the last of it. There is no stealing in this school. There never has been, and there never will be, do you understand?"

At that moment, Ameshin and Lily knew they would not be getting any help from Miss Warple in finding out who took the violin.

And it was not only Miss Warple who had already had enough of these two new girls, but the whole of Tregonwell House were wishing Lily, in particular, was not one of theirs. Lily's discredit put them bottom of the Winkton Abbey Cup before the term had even got going.

Having endured the longest Thursday of her life, Lily felt exhausted when she sat down at prep.

Not only was she trying to keep up with learning subjects which were too advanced for her age-group, she'd also been teased throughout lessons and at break times about her discredit. Plus, she was still hearing the odd comment and snigger about the toilet-roll-in-the-shoe incident.

The teasing did not help the fact that her heels were still red raw. All she wanted to do was stuff a roll of tissue inside her socks, but she daren't do it, in case someone spotted the loo roll again. Instead, she limped about, slipping her shoes off whenever she could.

Lily wiggled her toes under the table, losing concentration half-way through a maths problem which she couldn't solve, and she wondered if her blisters were meant to be a constant reminder that she was the poorest pupil in the school. Not that anyone had teased her about having no money. She wasn't sure if the others knew she was poor. *Perhaps everyone assumes you have money if you come to school here,* she thought. She hoped the assumption of wealth would last. Being teased any further was the last thing she needed.

By bedtime, Lily had hardly seen Ameshin all day. Miss Warple had banned the two of them from sitting together in lessons, and although Ameshin didn't have her violin, she still went and sat in the music room by herself at break-times and mimicked the best air violin she could muster. It was rather a sorry sight. At lunchtime, earlier that day, Lily had popped her head through the door to check Ameshin was all right. She was so engrossed in her imaginary playing she decided not to disturb her, even though she had come to discuss the violin theft.

Prep soon ended, and dinner came and went, and at last Lily and Ameshin were in their bottom bunks, waiting for Jinny, Laura and Claire to fall asleep.

"Amie, I've been watching people today, and thinking," Lily whispered into the darkness, hoping her friend was still awake.

"What have you been thinking?" said Ameshin.

"We need to narrow down our suspects to help figure out who might have your violin," said Lily.

"I agree. My top suspects are the head boy, Thomas Allen, and Mr Taplow, the music teacher," said Ameshin.

"Okay. Mine are that old caretaker, and someone whose name I can't say," said Lily.

"Why can't you say?" said Ameshin.

"In case she hears me," said Lily.

She clapped her hand over her silly mouth, knowing that if Jinny was listening, she might figure out Lily had been talking about her. Then Lily would be in for it.

Jinny snorted in her sleep, turning onto her side. Lily breathed easier, and Ameshin knew exactly why Lily had thought Jinny could be involved. Firstly, she was a vile excuse for a girl, and secondly, she wasn't in prep when she should have been yesterday evening, so she was up to something; and thirdly, when she came into their bedroom and caught them playing with the ghost-board, she had thrown her sports bag under her bed as soon as she'd come in. Anything could have been in that bag.

"What shall we do now?" said Ameshin.

"You follow your suspects, and I'll follow mine," said Lily.

"Good idea. Don't let them out of your sight, and make some notes so we can compare," said Ameshin.

"Yes, I will do. Don't worry, Amie, we'll get them," said Lily. "And we'll find your violin."

The girls drifted off to sleep, thinking about how they would catch the thief. The main suspects had been identified, and they were going to be watched, very closely indeed.

Chapter Five

The Followers

Ameshin found it no easy task to follow two people around, in secret, all day, every day, and make it to lessons on time, and fit in pretend violin practice, and attend prep and dinner.

She also found if you follow someone for long enough, you'll find out all sorts of things you would otherwise never have known. For instance, Mr Taplow always sang on the toilet, and Thomas Allen liked to read books about vegetables.

On a dreary Tuesday morning, after an hour of computing, and an hour of chemistry, Ameshin went looking for Thomas Allen. This was the fifth day she'd followed him like a shadow and not once had she seen any behaviour she could note as suspicious.

As usual it didn't take long for Ameshin to find the head boy at break time. His brown blazer made him stand out from everyone else in the school. Beneath a sunny blue sky, she sat down at the edge of the playing fields and pretended to read a book. Peering over the top of the pages, she watched Tom sitting and chatting with friends, on the main lawn. Tom hardly ever left the side of his girlfriend, Hannah Day, and he was just as close to his other friends, who Ameshin still held under high suspicion.

It must be a nice feeling, Ameshin thought, *to have loads of friends who look up to you. Perhaps Tom isn't the type to have stolen my violin.*

She also began to think playing detective wasn't much fun. *Perhaps I need to try something else to find my violin.* After that thought struck, Thomas Allen got up and made a move towards the main house, alone. Ameshin casually put her book into her bag, hurrying over to the main entrance, into which Tom had disappeared.

She hopped and skipped along to catch up. Her heart raced. She had been following Tom for so long now and this was the first time she'd seen him going anywhere, but to the loo, by himself.

Ameshin caught sight of Tom's foot vanishing around a corner. She followed as closely as she could. Any noise, or getting too close, or moving too fast, would get her caught, and she didn't think that following the head boy for suspicion of theft would do her any favours with Miss Warple.

It soon became clear, Tom was heading for the lockers. He was acting strangely, too. He stopped once and turned his head back to see if he was being followed. Ameshin had, by some stroke of luck, found herself too close behind her suspect, and a moment before his turning, ducked down behind a cabinet. The dark corridor was the perfect cover to follow behind, but the break-time silence made it difficult to move along without being heard.

As Tom reached the lockers, Ameshin stepped out of sight into a doorway, a few metres behind. Tom stopped, looking back once more. There was no one there, as far as he could see, but Ameshin was watching him. She willed him to try the lock of a locker. She didn't care who it was that had somehow managed to break into her locker, she just wanted to know where her violin was.

Tom double-checked both ways up and down the corridor. Ameshin had one eye peeping around the doorway, watching his every move. Tom walked on. To Ameshin's surprise, he walked straight past the lockers. *Where's he going?* she thought. *Why is he acting all suspicious if he isn't here to steal something?*

Tom placed his hand on the handle of a door beyond the lockers, checked both ways once more, and went inside. Ameshin had never noticed that door before. She thought it must be a closet, except why would the head boy be careful about being seen going into a closet.

She crept out from her hiding place, moving closer to the door. The paintings on the wall watched her creeping along. The silence of the hallway was broken only by Ameshin's heartbeat pounding with intrigue. She'd never done anything like this before. Her nerves were building up inside her stomach. Holding a breath inward, she skulked along, closer, and closer to the closet door. She reached her hand out for the door handle.

"Ameshin," a voice called from along the hall.

Ameshin leapt three feet into the air. By the time she'd landed, she'd realised the voice was Lily's and her fright had subsided somewhat. Lily stepped forward out of a dark doorway up the corridor.

"What are *you* doing here?" said Ameshin. "Why are you following Tom?"

"I'm not following Tom," said Lily.

"So, what are you doing here?" said Ameshin.

"I'm following Jinny. She went in there, two minutes ago, right before Tom did," said Lily.

A look of confusion struck Ameshin's face. She looked at the sign on the door. It was yellow with a picture of what looked like a bucket and brush on it. Ameshin had thought that this room was a closet, and she was right, it was the caretaker's cupboard.

"What shall we do?" said Lily.

"I brought my camera, in case I needed proof of something. I think we should get a photo of whatever is going on behind this door. Jinny and Tom are up to something. Neither of them were in prep the evening my violin got stolen, also what was Tom doing that night in the girls' boarding house anyway?" said Ameshin.

"You're right, they're up to something. Get your camera ready," said Lily.

Ameshin took a slim, portable camera from her blazer pocket. Lily took hold of the door handle and gently twisted it down. She teased the door open, just wide enough for Ameshin to slide the camera inside. A flash went off in the room. The girls hadn't expected that.

Tom shouted, "Hey, who's there?"

Lily and Ameshin fumbled about in the corridor. Lily slammed the door shut. There was nothing else for it, the girls sprinted and they didn't stop running until they got to their dorm.

Catching their breath, they started to laugh.

"I feel like a ninja," said Lily.

"Ninja's don't run, because they never get caught," said Ameshin.

"And they don't leave the flash on their secret camera's," said Lily. "What were they up to in there?"

Ameshin was already loading up the photo-viewer on her camera. The two girls watched a picture of a sand-timer filling and turning as the picture loaded. Then, it was there—a photograph that would change everything for Lily and Ameshin.

The picture showed Tom and Jinny locked at the lips, eyes closed, hands all over each other, and very much enjoying a secret romance.

The girls smiled at each other. They knew that neither the head boy, nor Jinny would like this photo to be seen by anyone. Not least because of Tom's girlfriend, or Jinny being two years younger, but the school rules were clear on PDA—'No public displays of affection'. A six-inch rule was in place between boys and girls. Opposite sexes were to remain six inches apart at all times. A photo like this would land both of them in a lot of trouble.

"It looks like we've just made some new friends," said Lily.

"I should've guessed from the way they looked at each other the other night. That, and the fact Tom was visiting our dorm, when he had no reason to. What will his girlfriend say?" said Ameshin.

"She might not have to find out," said Lily.

"We'll have to tell her, won't we?" said Ameshin.

"We'll keep this to ourselves. Just for now. Keep that photo safe. I won't feel so obliged to do as Jinny says from now on, that's for sure," said Lily, with a bright sparkle glimmering in her eye.

The school bell rang, break-time was over.

"I'm glad two of our suspects are ruled out. Come on, we've got music now, and then I'm back to following Mr Taplow," said Ameshin.

"I just hope we're following the right people, otherwise it could be anyone. Cover for me in music, will you? Tell Taplow I wasn't feeling well, and I've gone to see Matron Jackie. I'm going to find out what this caretaker is up to. I've seen him getting into a couple of old locks without a key, and I need to keep an eye him," said Lily.

"Don't get yourself into trouble," said Ameshin.

"Ninja," said Lily, striking a silly pose.

Ameshin shook her head, laughing, and the girls went their separate ways at the bottom of the stairs. Lily felt that missing a music lesson was essential so she could keep an eye on another main suspect. Although, following the caretaker, Mr Stoot, was a real test for her nerves, she found him to be altogether a very strange mannered man, and very slippery. When being followed, he somehow always managed to disappear, even when there was no way out of a room, and even when Lily was following him as closely as she could.

Lily wandered down the quiet corridors. She was getting to know the school very well with all the sneaking about. Upon passing each classroom, she ducked down below the window-line, so as not to get spotted and sent back to her lesson. Pretending to be a ninja was probably keeping her from being caught. But she had a ready-made alibi about not feeling well, in case a teacher saw her.

Mr Stoot, the caretaker, was nowhere to be found. Lily looked along all of the corridors in the main house. There was no sign of him. He wasn't in the food hall, and he wasn't in the staff room. Lily left the main house to have a look around the rest of the school grounds.

She shuffled along, tight to the outside walls.

Some classes were out on the fields doing PE, and some classes were in classrooms which were scattered around the grounds in some outside buildings. Lily decided it best to walk normally, instead of sneaking, so she didn't draw attention to herself if spotted by a nosey teacher or a busy-body prefect.

The dark entrance of the abbey loomed. She moved with caution towards the arched porch, listening hard to see if anyone might be inside before she entered. There was no sound, but for her own footsteps pressing softly on the flagstones.

She passed beneath the arched porchway and edged the abbey's giant oak door open, trying to stay silent.

Without the distraction of other pupils, Lily had the chance to appreciate the inside of this building, which was grand enough for God himself to visit anytime he was passing. Stone carved ceilings lurched high above. Golden ornaments dressed small alcoves dotted around the church. Ornate tapestries and marble sculptures told of the true wealth that had passed through over the history of Winkton Abbey.

Those who knew Lily's family would never have believed they had the means to send her to a school with its own abbey. Had she not seen the dedication put into saving their money, Lily wouldn't have believed it herself.

Walking into the abbey always made Lily wonder how she got so lucky.

"I've been watching you," a voice said.

Lily turned. Mr Stoot was piercing his dark eyes hard into hers. Lily said nothing. Partly from being scared, and partly from being caught.

"I've been watching you, watching me. And I can't think what you're expecting to see," said Mr Stoot.

Lily still couldn't speak. She stood still, gawping.

"I've got no choice but to take you to Miss Warple," said Mr Stoot. "Sneaking around during lesson times will not go unpunished at this school."

"Oh, please, no Mr Stoot. I'm sorry. I swear I am," said Lily, finding a desperate voice.

Mr Stoot wasn't having any of Lily's pleading. He had heard all of the excuses in the book whenever he'd caught someone out of class, and he was fed up with being fed lies and rubbish.

He marched Lily from the abbey and straight across the field, where everyone in lessons could see that Lily Thicke was in trouble once again.

Ameshin rushed to the window of the music room, fighting to the front of a nest of pupils who were fussing about someone being in trouble outside.

"Oh no," said Ameshin to herself when she saw. "Poor Lily."

Ameshin ran out of the classroom. Mr Taplow called her back, but she was long gone by the time he poked his head out of the door to enquire as to where she thought she was going.

Miss Warple opened her office door to see Mr Stoot with a firm hand on Lily's shoulder.

"Thicke, you again?" she said.

Lily smiled, which only made the situation worse.

Miss Warple bent down from her manly height, coming eye to eye with Lily.

"I had a wart once, right on the tip of my nose, which just wouldn't go away. You are rather reminding me of this old wart at the moment," she said, standing back up, sharply.

It seemed to Lily like Miss Warple had a telescopic body, which she could stretch up as high as she wanted to go. "What's the problem, Stoot?" she said.

"I found this one in the abbey, when she should have been in lessons, Miss Warple. She's been following me around for days, I'm sure of it," Mr Stoot said.

"Bring her inside," said Miss Warple.

Ameshin arrived out of breath.

"You as well…? I never had two warts on the end of my nose. I've a feeling you're both in this together. Let's see what you've got to say for yourselves, shall we?" said Miss Warple.

The girls promptly told Miss Warple everything about who they were following and why. Mr Taplow was summoned to the office, as he had been lied to about Lily going to see the matron, and his name had also been mentioned as a suspect in the case of the stolen violin. The only details the girls chose to leave out were those about the photo of Tom and Jinny — that was a secret to be kept for another day.

Miss Warple listened well, and she encouraged the girls to get their concerns off their chests. Once they had finished, Miss Warple stood behind her desk and pushed her great knuckles hard into the surface.

"I cannot tell you how many school rules you have both broken in your first couple of weeks at Winkton Abbey," Miss Warple said. Her eyes began to boil. "I have no choice but to suspend you both for one week. I ask that you leave the school premises this evening, before dinner."

The girls' mouths dropped open in horror.

"But, miss, we've been completely honest with you!" said Lily.

"Honesty falls from the tongues of fools," said Miss Warple.

"I've always been taught to be honest," said Lily.

Miss Warple hissed and smiled at the same time. "Your father will be called shortly, Ms Thicke, and he will be summoned to pick you up. Ms Chi, as you are from overseas a different arrangement will be made with your father for your exclusion."

"Please, miss, my father doesn't know that my violin has been stolen. It wouldn't do much good for me to tell him, until I know for sure I can't find it," said Ameshin.

"Your. Stupid. Violin. Was. Not. Stolen. You will stop these accusations at once. Your own carelessness must not be blamed on others. You have been following pupils, and the head boy, and teachers around the school. Who do you think you are? Your father will be called and told about your behaviour. That is final. Lily, you can walk home, or be picked up by someone. Ameshin, I want you waiting for further instructions in the food hall," said Miss Warple.

She waved the girls out of her room as she picked up the telephone.

Ameshin and Lily left Miss Warple's office in a daze, going straight up to their dorm.

Opening her suitcase, Lily wanted to say how sorry she was about everything. Ameshin looked more shocked than the moment she found her violin had been taken. The two of them remained silent. At the bottom of the stairway, they went their separate ways without so much as a glance at each other as they began their sentence of one week's suspension.

After sitting outside of the school's main house for an hour, Lily looked up to see a car she had ridden in many times, each time of which, had been a joyous occasion. This time, a bittersweet feeling washed over her. She was glad to see her Uncle Peter had come to collect her from school and take her home. The downside of that was he was a policeman. When Lily got into the back of the police car it made Lily feel even more guilty than she already did. Her uncle might as well have put the flashing lights on and sounded the sirens as he drove away from Winkton Abbey school. Not that he needed to, plenty of people were already taking an interest in who was sitting in the back.

Chapter Six
Stranger and Stranger

"I'm sorry," Lily said. "I know I shouldn't have followed the caretaker."

"You've said sorry enough times now, Lily," said Mrs Thicke.

"And you've only been home for an hour," said Mr Thicke.

They were sitting in the lounge. The 1960's floral decoration on the walls and sofas looked nearly as sorry as Lily did. Both were in need of some tender loving care.

"You're not going to shout anymore?" said Lily.

"Not now I know the truth," said Mr Thicke.

"It's common sense that you were trying to help your friend. There's no harm in that," said Mrs Thicke.

"Miss Warple will see it that way soon enough," said Mr Thicke. "I'll go to the school and talk to her."

"No, don't. I'll end up in more trouble if you do that," said Lily.

Lily's father looked crestfallen. He thought that would help, but he didn't know who he was dealing with in Miss Warple. Lily was glad he didn't press the matter.

Regardless of her parents' understanding, Lily was on her best behaviour whilst at home. She did all of the washing up after dinner. She cleaned every window in the house and the mirrors. She went about trimming rows of seemingly endless hedges in the garden, and burning the waste, and weeding the paths, all while her father put his feet up. She baked apple crumble, and took care of the laundry, while her mother read her favourite book. Mr and Mrs Thicke kept on telling her she really didn't need to do any of it, but helping out was all Lily felt she could do to stop herself from feeling so bad.

The suspension week shot by with keeping so busy. When it came to going back to school on the Sunday evening, Lily was dreading the return.

Not because she didn't want to go back. It was more of an issue with the arranged transport. In fact, it's fair to say that she might rather have walked back to school than return in the same fashion as she'd left. That being in her Uncle's police car. Usually, Lily would have really enjoyed being picked up by her uncle. Upon request, he would never fail to put the lights on and race through traffic to wherever they were going. But, being picked up and dropped off at school in a police car, when you'd been home for a week's suspension, was more embarrassing than being spotted with toilet roll hanging out the back of your shoe on the first day of school.

At six o'clock on Sunday evening, Uncle Peter's police car pulled up outside of the school's main house.

Lily's worst fears had come true.

Dozens of boarders huddled around to see her stepping out of the police car. Someone must have been keeping watch at the front of school, waiting for her, and had somehow let the others know she was arriving.

When leaving in the police car last week, Lily had noticed Bethany Cahill and Anna Tropp taking a keen interest as to who was sitting inside. They'd run over and bent down to get a good look. Lily had wondered who they would gather up to have a laugh when she returned.

As if it wasn't bad enough being in the back of the police car, the child-lock was on. Lily's uncle stepped out of the car and opened the back door for her. How many criminals had he done that for. That's what Lily felt like, a criminal. She was ashamed. She couldn't look at anybody. She smiled to her Uncle Peter. He watched the poor girl disappear inside the manor house, wondering if he wouldn't be back before long to take her home again.

The crowd dispersed as the excitement of a police car being at school petered out.

Lily walked into her dorm. Laura and Claire said hello, but the strange thing was that Izzy was lying on Ameshin's bed.

"Izzy, what are you doing in here?" said Lily.

"Sorry to tell you this, Lily, but they swapped me and Ameshin around," said Izzy.

Lily could just believe it. Miss Warple had already separated them in class, why wouldn't she separate them in their dorms, too. Lily sank into her bunk without saying a word.

"You've really done it this time, Thicko," said Jinny. "I think the ghost was right, someone will get expelled this year. The smart money is on you."

Lily ignored Jinny, curling up on her bottom bunk. When the others had gone down for dinner she stayed in bed where she cried and fell asleep.

*

It was a new day. Lily woke up feeling much brighter. Over breakfast, which consisted of jam, toast, and tea, she decided to put the past behind her and get back to learning. She hurried off to lessons without drinking her cup of tea.

The early morning sun was shining through the classroom window and straight into Lily's eyes. She was one of the first into the classroom, and being early for her lesson she sat at the front for a change. She decided that as well as putting the past behind her, she was also going to make up for all of her bad behaviour. From now on she was going to be the perfect pupil.

Lily tried to catch Ameshin's eye as she walked into the room. It seemed as if Ameshin hadn't seen her, but Lily knew Ameshin was much too aware of her surroundings to fool her into believing that. Lily didn't know it, but as well as being banned from sitting next to each other, and being removed from the same dorm, Ameshin now wasn't even allowed to speak to Lily. Her father had forbidden it.

Ameshin took a seat at the back of the class, keeping her head down, despite Lily's best efforts to attract her attention. Throughout the lesson Lily kept looking back at her friend, hoping for a glimpse of a smile, or any sign they were still friends. There was nothing.

For the rest of the day, Lily and Ameshin avoided each other. It was the loneliest and longest day either of them had had since starting school. Ameshin used the extra time to practice with her new violin, which she hated, and she finished off her homework in prep extra quick, at which point she went straight back to her practice.

In the dining room, Lily was eating her dinner alone when one of her classmates came over and sat beside her. A boy called Benjamin Sawkins. Lily remembered back to seeing him on the very first day when she'd thought they'd make good friends. She hadn't really spoken to him, or to anyone else, since the first day of term. She hadn't needed to, since she and Ameshin had become best friends. Now she thought she might never make another friend ever again.

"Lily," said Ben, "is it really true about the violin going missing out of the locker?"

Lily didn't know if someone had sent him over for some kind of trick, or a joke. She avoided answering the question.

"Why do you care?" said Lily, acting colder than she would have liked.

"I think someone took something of mine, too," he said.

Lily perked up. She slid closer to Ben. "What was taken?" she said.

"I'm pretty sure I left my watch in my locker, but I couldn't tell anyone about it. Not after you two got into so much trouble for accusing people of stealing," said Ben.

"And it was stolen?" Lily said.

Ben nodded. "My mother bought me the watch when I turned 10. It was a Rolex. She'll be ever so angry with me for losing it," he said.

"You didn't *lose* it. And don't think for one minute that you did," said Lily. "There is a thief at the school, I know it."

"Do you think you can help get it back?" said Ben, raising a faint smile.

Lily thought about her answer very carefully. She'd already gotten into trouble for trying to help Ameshin. This was really none of her business, but she couldn't stand for stealing, and she couldn't leave a mystery unsolved. The ghost had said that someone was at the school who shouldn't be, and Lily was going to find them, no matter what it took.

"Tell me everything that happened, and we'll see what we can do," said Lily, being as hush hush as she could.

Ben abided by speaking in the same hush hush fashion. "I was given a detention by Mrs Williams, last

Wednesday," he said. "It was my own silly fault, I put on Robert Grooms' blazer after PE, and went off to prep wearing it. His blazer had the wrong name in it see. Benjamin Reeves, I think the label said, it must have been second-hand. I saw the Benjamin part and thought it was mine. Robert kicked up a stink and got me in trouble."

"Then what happened?" said Lily.

"Mrs Williams said I'd put Robert's blazer on and run off to wind him up, then she gave me a Friday lunch detention. So, come Friday, I knew I'd have a lot of writing lines to do and I didn't want to wear my heavy watch. I took it off and locked it in my locker. I often put it in there. I thought it would be safe enough. I went to detention, but when I came back my watch was gone," said Ben, his face sinking with sadness.

"Will you tell the school in assembly that your watch was stolen?" said Lily.

"I don't want to get into any trouble," said Ben.

Lily could understand that. "Who took your detention on Friday, out of curiosity?" she said.

"It was Thomas Allen, the head boy, and Ray Perkins, the detention monitor," said Ben.

"Was Tom there with you the whole time?" said Lily.

"Yes, he was, for the whole hour," said Ben.

"I can't promise anything, Ben. Leave it with me. I'll be keeping an eye out for anything out of the ordinary," said Lily.

Ben left Lily to finish her dinner. She didn't eat another mouthful, she was too busy thinking about suspects. The craziest suspect that popped into her head was Miss Warple herself. She was being so adamant that stealing didn't happen at the school, and she refused to look into the claim. Yet, if a boy walks around with his shirt hanging out he is handed a detention. It didn't quite make sense to take so much notice of the small things and ignore the serious things.

The problem was, Lily couldn't go following people again, she needed to be cleverer than that, but there were no clues, and she had no idea who it could be.

Perhaps we need to lay a trap, she thought. *It would have to be top secret, I might have to do this alone.*

In the dorm after dinner, Jinny was teasing Lily about her suspension, and giving Lily her views on how she thought people should know how to behave coming to a school like this, which didn't include snooping around. Lily took the horrid words on the chin.

You just wait, Jinny Green, you'll not be so nasty when I tell you what I have, Lily was picturing the photo of Jinny and Tom's embrace.

Izzy, on the other hand, was being much kinder to Lily. She was telling her about being made captain of the girls' hockey team, and about her older sister, Emily, winning two credits for her performances in last week's hockey and netball matches.

"It's funny you know, Lily, your discredit gave everyone the motivation to try their hardest to win everything they could. Being bottom for the last couple of weeks hasn't been fun at all. The girls in Drake house gave us a really hard time," said Izzy.

"Sorry about that. I swear I'm being honest about the violin going missing. Miss Warple just didn't want to hear it," said Lily.

"What do you think happened to Ameshin's violin?" Laura said, poking her head down from the top bunk.

"She lost it and tried to blame someone else for it," said Jinny.

"I think she's telling the truth," said Claire.

"Me too," said Laura. "Ameshin's one of the smartest girls I know. She's telling the truth all right."

Lily had no idea that they believed the violin had been stolen. She brightened up immediately.

"What do you think of Mr Stoot? I've seen him breaking into a lock of an old door, and he's very strange, don't you think?" said Lily.

"He gives me the creeps," said Izzy.

"Oh, he's okay. He helped me rescue one of the school ferrets down from a tree last year," said Claire.

"You'd better be careful who you're accusing, Thicko. One more mess up from you, and you're out," said Jinny.

"Perhaps you and Tom Allen could help me solve the case?" said Lily.

The girls giggled. Jinny looked sharply at Lily.

"What's Tom Allen got to do with anything?" said Jinny.

"Aren't you two really good friends?" said Lily.

Jinny somehow knew that Lily had found out about her and Tom, or had maybe seen something. She backed down immediately.

"You're better off just leaving it alone. It's not your violin that went missing, and this thief isn't exactly rampant," said Jinny.

"But the thief has stolen again," said Lily.

The girls didn't believe it.

"No, when?" said Laura.

"Last Friday. Poor Benjamin Sawkins had a watch taken from his locker. Someone is stealing at this school and I'm going to find them," said Lily.

Chapter Seven

A Class Outing

Many days went by without Lily and Ameshin speaking. In fact, Lily didn't speak to anyone much other than Ben and Izzy. And Ameshin only spoke to the teachers when she was asked a question. Both girls were struggling to come to terms with how their first few weeks at their new school was turning out.

Nonetheless, Lily was still turning up to lessons early, and sitting at the front, and keeping up the appearance of being the perfect pupil. She had even been placed third best in the class in an English literature test. She was only beaten by Ameshin, and Georgina Boyce, the cleverest girl in the year. It was fair to say that managing to stay out of trouble was serving Lily well. Although, she hadn't let the business of the thefts escape her mind altogether. She continued to watch *everyone* as they went about the school. She was determined to spot any signs of *the one who shouldn't be there*.

A disorderly tail of pupils were presently piling into the abbey for morning assembly. Lily wanted to talk to Ameshin, to tell her about Ben's watch. Assembly was the only place she figured she could fix the chance. And the only place they weren't officially banned from sitting together. Although, it was a risk, since Miss Warple would be standing right in front of them.

Lily spotted long dark hair, draping down the back of the slight figure that was Ameshin's. She pushed past a few others to get in behind her. Ameshin took her seat, shuffling along the pew up close to the wall, and unbeknownst to her, Lily plonked herself down in the seat beside her.

"Hi, Amie," she said.

Ameshin looked surprised. "I'm not allowed to talk to you," she whispered, on edge, as if her father was somewhere in the abbey, spying on her.

"I just wanted to let you know I'm still on the case," said Lily.

"You need to drop it, Lily. I have a new violin now, there's nothing we can do anyway," said Ameshin.

"How is your new violin?" said Lily.

"It plays just fine," said Ameshin.

"Well, just fine is, just fine, I guess," said Lily, being able to tell Ameshin still wanted her old violin back.

The conversation was cut short by the teachers making their way into the abbey. This meant everyone had to be quiet and stand up.

Miss Warple whipped up to her lectern. Every last pupil was standing up straight by the time she looked up. They then all sat back down again, as soon as they were told to do so. Then everyone stood back up again, when they were told to do so.

The morning hymn was sung, and the school children sat patiently, listening to Miss Warple babbling on about sports reports; and who the best sportsmen were; and school values that weren't being obeyed stringently enough; and the good work that the ferret club in the fourth year were doing with culling rabbits and moles for the good of the sports fields.

"And now we come to the Winkton Abbey Cup," said Miss Warple. "It is nearly half-term, and nearly half-way through the autumn term. At this point, Drake sits in first place with 20 credits. Edison is in second with 18 credits. Tregonwell in third with 17. Hardy are in fourth place with 15. May I remind you that winning the WAC for your house is an honour that adds to your character development here at Winkton Abbey. Always try your best and you can do no wrong. Misbehave and be lazy, and you will go nowhere," she said.

Miss Warple left it at that. She sent a solid stare to Lily and Ameshin to let them know she'd seen them sitting together.

The stare put Ameshin back on edge. She really didn't want to get into any more trouble than she already had. Fortunately, Miss Warple didn't raise the issue in front of the school. She walked out of assembly with the teachers following behind. The pupils soon bumbled along out of the abbey, dispersing to lessons.

Outside of the abbey, Mr Khan, the biology teacher, came bounding over to the third years, full of positive energy. "All third years, hurry to your dorms and lockers, please. Get your jackets, wellies, writing pads, and whatever else you need for a trip to the river. Come and meet over at the minibus. As quickly as you can please!" he said.

Lily, Ben, Ameshin, Izzy, Robert, Georgina, and the rest of the third year classes ran to get their things. Outside of the sports hall they hopped onto the school's largest minibus. A long, white Mercedes. The Winkton Abbey crest was proudly painted on each side.

The third years were bouncing about, a tad over excited at being taken on a surprise trip to the river. Much more exciting than the scheduled maths and biology lessons they were missing.

Lily sat at the front of the bus. She regretted doing so, once everyone began to walk straight past her. She understood people thought she was trouble, and they didn't want to get mixed up with her. She hoped this line of thinking wouldn't last for long, but that's how it was, for now.

A few rows behind her, Lily was pleased to see Ben and Ameshin sitting together. She often hoped the three of them would one day become friends, if Ameshin would ever speak to her again.

The last person to get onto the bus was Robert Groom. Lily couldn't stand him ever since he'd embarrassed her in front of the whole school on her first day. He sat down heavily, squashing into Lily's side. It seemed as if good manners were one thing his father had forgotten to pay for.

"I've never asked what you were doing standing outside the gates when you arrived at boarding school. Did your car break down, or something?" Robert said, to Lily.

"I walked to school," said Lily. "My family doesn't own a car."

"Oh, well how far did you walk?" said Robert.

"Dad said it was about fourteen miles," said Lily.

"Gosh," said Robert. He smiled at the feat. "That's ridiculous. And pretty amazing, too," he said.

That wasn't the reaction Lily was expecting. Surely he wanted to mock her for not having a car. Surely he wanted to laugh that she had to walk so far to school when he had been chauffer driven.

"Was that the reason for all the loo roll in your shoe?" said Robert.

Lily nodded. "My Mum put the tissues in my shoes, because I had really bad blisters," said Lily.

"That was funny though," said Robert, smiling.

Lily didn't think so.

Mr Khan interrupted, jumping onto the bus. "Are we all here then?" He looked around at a full bus of thirty seats. "Righto, we're off to the river for a live biology class," he said.

Incessant chattering carried on as the bus weaved down country lanes. Lily though, didn't want to start any further conversations with Robert. She sat with her head turned away from him, looking out of the window.

Lily knew these country lanes well. She'd walked and cycled around most of them. The thought struck her, that if her family had owned a car, and had always driven around these roads instead of walking, she would probably never have noticed the little things that made the countryside so beautiful to her. Such as the village signs with black iron letters showing quirky names like Nutford, Steepleton, and Fiddleford; and trickling streams along the sides of the roads; and stone-built cottages with thatched roofs, tucked away at the bottom of lawned gardens, only visible through tiny gaps in the hedgerows; and the bees in the flowers collecting pollen; and the sound of sheep as you went strolling past a farm.

Indeed, the minibus whizzed past all of this, without any notice from the other children. Some of those who hailed from towns and cities probably thought the countryside was made up of boring trees and fields, but Lily knew the natural world was full of endless intrigue. She could never be bored with it.

The minibus pulled off the road, parking up on a patch of grass.

Mr Khan hopped out. "Come on then," he said. "Let's get exploring."

He was trying his best to instil a sense of excitement into those who didn't find any excitement in the great outdoors.

Lily found they were somewhere she'd not been before. She took in her surroundings. A flour mill, tall and imposing, was peeking through the branches of an old oak tree. The water wheel looked to Lily like it could still do a hard day's work, hundreds of years after it had been mounted. The mill lake had collected an autumn sea of leaves, brown, red and orange, making the grass and pond merge together as one. Autumn was in full fall, and where the water's surface was visible, it sat as still as glass, reflecting shades of grey from the moody sky above.

Lily thought it was lovely to be outside of school, and out in the open for a real lesson. It started to spit with rain. The glass-surfaced water began to shatter. Everyone hurried to put on their jackets.

Mr Khan moved about the children handing out empty plastic food bags, and clipboards.

"Get into pairs everyone. As we go along, you'll see blackberries and raspberries, ripe for picking. Collect as many as you can for the fruit crumble at school this evening. Don't eat too many yourselves," he said. "And your partner, with the clipboard, must note down as much wildlife, and flora and fauna as you can both identify. Off we go."

Mr Khan led the third years along the river, beneath a light spattering of rain. Lily couldn't believe it, she'd been paired up with Robert *again*.

She'd never spent longer than ten seconds with him before, and now she was going to spend most of the day with him. Lily made sure she had the clipboard, and she kept herself busy, scanning the land for squirrels, and mice, and water shrews, and butterflies, and rabbits, and swans, and geese, and warblers, robins, and tits. She was determined to have the best list of wildlife to give to Mr Khan by the end of the day. She even added notes about what the animals were doing around the river at this time of year. If she hadn't spotted the actual animal yet, she made a note of the habitat belonging to that animal, and the various runs and trails which she had spotted.

"Do you think we have much more walking to do before lunch?" said Robert.

"I expect there's quite some way yet," said Lily.

"My feet are getting wet. I've got a hole coming through the bottom of my shoe," said Robert.

Lily didn't have much sympathy for him. "Where are your wellies?" she said. "We're all wearing our wellies, see?"

"I forgot them," said Robert. "I can be clumsy like that."

What's this? Lily thought. *Robert Groom is being humble. Maybe he isn't such a bent-twig after all. Maybe he's just a bit of a clutz. Was I wrong? He's never said anything horrible to me. He's only bumped into me a couple of times, and the whole toilet roll incident would have been funny for anyone else but me.*

"What does your father do to be so wealthy, Robert?" said Lily.

"He's a businessman, in London. Stocks and shares, or something like that," said Robert. "What about your parents?"

"My father's a farmer, on Dillervale Farm, and my mother is a nurse at a doctor's surgery," said Lily.

"Do you own the farm?" said Robert.

Lily smiled. "No, we don't own anything much at all. They're both on the minimum wage, I hear them say," she said.

"You own a pair of wellies. At least that's something," said Robert.

Lily didn't want to like Robert. He had made her new life at her dream school start off as a nightmare. Despite this, she warmed up to him the more they spoke. She got to know that he liked the outdoors, mainly when it was dry; he wasn't brilliant at sports; he didn't excel in anything; and he didn't boast about much at all, not even about money. In fact, Robert Groom was just an average boy with a good sense of humour, and that was why he'd found it so funny when he saw the toilet roll stuffed into the back of Lily's shoes. He never said sorry about making the whole school laugh at her, but Lily forgave him anyway. She actually enjoyed spending time with him, and collecting berries, and spotting fish, and listing all types of trees from ash to beech, to birch and oak, as they went along the river.

The minibus home was a lot quieter than the journey had been out to the river. There were some tired legs, and some wet heads, and a lot of berries to go into Mrs Plumley's crumble. The children handed their clipboards to Mr Khan. He did a count up on the way home, and when they arrived back he announced that Lily and Robert had the highest count for listing wildlife, trees, and flowers. He gave them both half a credit. Lily was made up for receiving a reward, she began to think that everything was beginning to change for her.

Maybe I should give up on trying to solve who the thief is, she thought. *Maybe I'm better off staying out of trouble.*

Chapter Eight
Being Wrong

Lily missed Ameshin.

There was no-one else with which she could fill a void of interesting conversation. She was getting along well with Robert, Izzy, and Ben, but Ameshin still wouldn't talk to her. Ameshin's silence was the only thing that kept Lily's hunt for the thief alive. She felt terribly sorry about Ben's birthday watch being stolen, and she did want to find that as well, but that was at least replaceable. Ameshin's violin was a real one off, and Lily was always thinking that if she somehow got the violin back, then they might become friends again. *It's been weeks since it went missing, though,* Lily thought, *I wonder if the violin is even still at the school?*

Lily was bursting to know who the thief was, and why the ghost had said they shouldn't be at the school. She constantly asked herself who it could be. The thief was all she could think about during her art lesson, the final lesson before the half-term holiday.

Whilst painting a pretty cottage with oil on canvas, Lily's thoughts rolled away from who the thief was. Her thoughts switched to thinking about her suspension, two weeks previous, and why she'd been foolish enough to be honest with Miss Warple. She'd learnt very early on that Miss Warple's punishment system was unduly harsh. As much as she disliked the headmistress, her stance on discipline had most definitely taught Lily something; and that something was, if she was going to sneak around and follow other people, she needed to do it quietly, and without anyone knowing.

Lily quite enjoyed art and making things out of bits and bobs. When she was younger her mother taught her it did no good to throw old things away when they can be upcycled and sold on, or used as something else entirely. That was what Lily was going to do to keep herself busy over the half-term.

Her mother had a collection of old chests of drawers, dressers, mirrors, and desks at home. She and Lily would spend the half-term sanding them down, painting and sprucing them up, to be sold on as good as new. This year, every penny made was going towards the Thicke's family Christmas fund.

With all of the furniture Lily had to work on over the half-term, she would be helping to pay for this year's tree and decorations, and turkey, with all of the trimmings as well. Lily could not wait for Christmas to come around. She loved the morning frosts, and the flashing lights in windows, and the thought of Santa flying around the world delivering presents all in one night. Most of all, for this year though, she was looking forward to seeing Ameshin playing her violin in the Christmas concert at the abbey.

Such nice thoughts were flowing through her mind as Lily painted tiny leaves laying on the grass in front of her cottage. That reminded her she shouldn't get too excited just yet, it was still autumn and Christmas was a little way off. The weather had only just started getting cold.

"Hey, Thicko," Jinny called through the art room door. "You didn't tell me your parents were on minimum wage, you loser. I knew you didn't deserve to be here. You're just not good enough for this school."

"That's enough of that, Jinny Green. Apologise to Lily right now, please," said Miss Packham, the art teacher.

Jinny walked off laughing. Miss Packham shook her head. She was one of those teachers that didn't do anything about anything, which was why Jinny laughed and walked away.

Lily had known it was only a matter of time before she was teased about money, and she could have guessed that it would be Jinny to mouth off about it first.

It must have been Robert, laughing at me behind my back. He is as bad as I thought. And that Jinny doesn't deserve to be here, she's plain horrid, she's the one skiving classes and being a complete nit. That's it, thought Lily. *Jinny shouldn't be here, like the ghost said—****Use your eyes, you will see, someone here, who should not be.*** *Maybe it is Jinny after all. She's mean enough to be a thief, and I never did get to follow her properly.*

Lily looked about the class for Robert. He wasn't there. Lucky for him. She wanted to throw a few choice words at him.

"Miss Packham, do you know where Robert Groom is?" Lily asked.

"Oh, that boy is such a wonderful artist," said Miss Packham.

"He is?" said Lily.

"I'm just marking some of his work now. Look at this sketch of Constable's Mill," Miss Packham said, holding up his work.

Lily wasn't exactly interested in Robert's sketch of a mill, but she took a look to humour Miss Packham. "That's very nice. Do you know where he is?" she said again.

"I believe he's gone home early. I saw a taxi arrive for him before the start of the lesson," said Miss Packham.

"Thanks, miss," said Lily.

Lily's words with Robert would have to wait. One thing Lily didn't want to wait for was saying goodbye to Ameshin. She stood up, without asking permission, and she went over to see Ameshin. Miss Packham let it slide, not least because she hated to restrict the children from doing as they pleased, but it was also the last Friday of half-term, and she thought everyone should leave in a happy mood.

"Have a good half-term, won't you," said Lily.

"Thanks. I expect I'll be practicing," said Ameshin.

"Where are you going for the week?" asked Lily.

"I'm going nowhere," said Ameshin, concentrating on a delicate paint-stroke.

"You're staying at the school? For the holiday? Don't be silly," said Lily.

"I'm not being silly. My parents are in Tokyo and I have nowhere else to go. Besides, it'll be nice and quiet for my practice," said Ameshin.

A thought struck Lily. She wondered if Ameshin could come to her house for the week. She stopped herself from saying anything, thinking that Ameshin wouldn't want to stay with her, after all she only lived in a bungalow, and Ameshin probably lived in a palace in Japan. But then she thought about everything they could do together.

"Come and stay with me, Amie. Please come and stay with me—won't you? It'd be great," said Lily.

"My father wouldn't allow that. I'm not even supposed to be speaking with you," said Ameshin.

"If he said yes though, would you come and stay?" asked Lily.

Ameshin nodded and smiled.

"If your father never knew about it, would you come and stay?"

Ameshin nodded harder and smiled more.

Lily sprinted out of the room. "Sorry, miss, I've got to go."

Miss Packham attempted to stop Lily with a feeble raising of a finger. She backed down when she realised Lily was already half way down the corridor.

Lily ran all the way to Miss Warple's office.

When she got there, she drew a deep breath, and knocked on the door.

"Come," Miss Warple's voice shook through the walls.

Lily opened the door, stepped inside, and closed the door behind her.

"Thicke. The wart hath returned. To what do I owe this displeasure?" said Miss Warple.

Lily was getting used to Miss Warple's remarks by now. They were infuriating, but at least she knew what to expect. Lily didn't dwell on it.

"Can Ameshin come and stay with me at half-term please, Miss Warple? She's top in almost all of her classes. We've both knuckled down since we were suspended, and we've forgotten all about the violin going missing nonsense," said Lily.

"Let me tell you something, young Lily. Ameshin's father does not want her hanging around with you, and I can't say I'm at all surprised," said Miss Warple.

"How many people are staying on at school to look after Ameshin?" said Lily.

"There will be myself, Mrs Plumley, and Matron Jackie at the school at all times," said Miss Warple.

"For one person? Wouldn't you all like to have a holiday, too? If Ameshin was at mine, you could all have the week off," said Lily.

Miss Warple did rather like the idea of a week away from seeing any children. "What about Ms Chi's father?" Miss Warple asked.

"You could call him," said Lily. "Although, Tokyo is eight hours ahead of us. That makes it 1am, and you probably wouldn't want to wake him up."

Miss Warple took a moment to think. Her wrinkles danced about her forehead. "No, I wouldn't want to wake him at that hour. I will write a permission note for Ameshin, and she will stay with you for the week," said Miss Warple, scribbling away on a pad.

"Oh, thank you, Miss Warple. That really is wonderful of you," said Lily.

Miss Warple handed the note over. "You two little warts will be good, won't you?" she said.

"Yes, miss. Of course, miss," said Lily.

The end of lesson bell rang. It was officially half-term. Lily sprinted back to art class, arriving as everyone else was leaving.

She shoved the note under Ameshin's nose.

Her smile grew as the news sank in that she wouldn't be alone for the week. And, although Ameshin knew her father wouldn't like it, she was certain he would never find out anyway.

The two girls were finally back together and instantly got to catching up on everything that had happened since they'd been suspended.

Lily caught sight of Ben in the corridor.

"Bye, Ben," Lily called across the hallway, through a crowd of hurrying children.

Ben stopped to let the crowds pass. "Have a good week. I don't suppose you've had any more ideas on this thief? I'll have to tell my parents about my watch, which I'm not looking forward to," he said.

"Sorry, Ben, I've not got much to go on. The thief is too smart for me at the moment," said Lily.

"Hey, is it true you don't have a car?" said Ben.

Lily blushed. "Yes, that's true," she turned to Ameshin. "Oh, that's what I was going to say, Ameshin, it's quite a walk to my house," she said.

"That's why I was asking," said Ben. "I'll get my dad to drop you off at your house. It's the least I can do for you even thinking about helping me find my watch." He grinned, hoping the girls would take him up on his offer.

Usually, Lily would not have accepted. She disliked accepting help from anyone when she knew she could do something by herself. But, the walk home would take the best part of four and a half hours, and that was at a brisk pace; and the walk would yield some rather large blisters, which would no doubt hinder the half-term fun; and she and Ameshin wouldn't be home until gone ten that evening. A car journey would take no more than twenty minutes. It was an easy decision.

"Thank you, Ben, are you sure he wouldn't mind?" said Lily.

"Go and get your bags and meet me out the front. My dad is the one with the Hummer, sorry about the colour of it," said Ben. He ran off, all excited to be giving a lift to two of the biggest rebels in school. Not that either Lily or Ameshin would ever have thought of themselves as rebels.

Lily walked into her dorm to fetch her bags, and a soft toy hit her in the face as she entered. Jinny was throwing things around the room, crying, and screaming, and moaning. *"Where is it? Where is it? Where is it?"* she kept on saying.

The other girls cowered on their bunks.

"What's wrong with her?" Lily asked Izzy.

"She's lost a necklace," said Izzy.

Jinny tipped her hair-brush basket out onto the bed. "Someone's stolen it. I didn't lose it," she said.

"When did it go missing?" said Lily.

"You took it! You took it, didn't you? To sell on so you can afford to come here!" said Jinny.

"I did no such thing," said Lily.

"Calm down, Jinny. When did it go missing?" said Laura.

"I can't calm down. Someone very important gave me that necklace. I took it off this morning and left it under my pillow. The door has been locked all day, only you lot have access to the room," said Jinny.

"Where were you when it went missing?" Lily asked. "And did it go missing before or after you teased me in the art room?"

"It's none of your business where I was," said Jinny.

Lily knew exactly where she'd been. *Saying goodbye to Thomas Allen before half-term is where you were,* Lily thought to herself.

"Wait, didn't Lily say that Mr Stoot can open locks without a key?" said Laura.

"Yes. And I saw him on this floor over lunchtime, when I came back up to finish packing my things," said Claire.

"It has to be him," said Laura. "Like Izzy said before, he gives me the creeps." She shuddered at the thought of the old caretaker.

At that moment Jinny stormed out of the room.

"Where are you going?" Lily called after her.

"To see Miss Warple," said Jinny.

Even though they were about to leave for home, the girls didn't want to miss this. Izzy, Lily, Claire and Laura skipped along the corridor keeping up with Jinny. She nearly broke down Miss Warple's door when she got there. She didn't so much as knock, but banged on the door and barged straight in. Miss Warple was sitting keenly at her desk.

"Jinny Green, is there something the matter?" said Miss Warple.

Jinny slammed the door. The girls listened to ranting, but couldn't tell the two voices apart at times. Shouting went back and forth. Lily thought that Jinny had some nerve going into Miss Warple's office like that. The girls heard Jinny telling Miss Warple to call Mr Stoot and get him to the office.

"How does she get away with it?" said Lily.

"Didn't you know?" said Laura.

"Miss Warple is Jinny's aunt," said Izzy.

That explained a lot to Lily.

The office fell silent, and the girls couldn't hear a word.

Mr Stoot walked up to the door and knocked. He sneered at the girls. At least it looked like a sneer, it might have been a smile, it was hard to tell.

"Come in," Miss Warple cried.

Mr Stoot, the caretaker, might as well have walked into a wasps' nest and put the queen right on the tip of his tongue. A torrent of abuse and accusations were tossed at him from two of the nastiest mouths Lily had ever encountered. He didn't last long inside and when he came out, he was trembling. Off he walked in the direction of the main door, and he didn't look back.

"Poor Mr Stoot," said Lily.

"Don't you think he deserved it?" said Laura.

"No one knows for sure that he was the thief. Where's the evidence?" said Lily. "No necklace, no watch, or no violin have been found. Firing him hasn't achieved anything."

Jinny strolled out with a smile on her face, and Miss Warple told the girls to stop hanging around outside her office. On the way back to the dorm, Jinny told the girls that Mr Stoot denied stealing her necklace. She told them that he'd said he was near their room, fitting some lightbulbs in the girls' hallway. Jinny added that she knew that was just another lie.

"Miss Warple made the right decision, getting rid of him. He's older than the floorboards in this place," said Jinny.

Lily felt terrible for the man.

She said goodbye to the girls, except for Jinny, and she hurried down to the main carpark to find Ben and Ameshin.

Ben's dad's Hummer was big and bold. A sunshine yellow that was unmissable. Lily could see why Ben would apologise about the colour of it, although she thought it was magnificent. A huge yellow Hummer was certainly better than being picked up in a police car.

As soon as she climbed into the car, Lily told Ben and Ameshin everything that had happened. Ben's dad drove along merrily as the story was told.

"So, Mr Stoot *is* the thief then," said Ben.

"We can't be sure of that, there's no evidence," said Lily.

"No one's found my watch then?" said Ben.

Ben's father lifted an eyebrow. He was listening to all of the school gossip, remembering back to when he'd been at school. "What's that about your watch, Ben?" said Mr Sawkins.

Ben's heart felt like it had been sucked out through the Hummer's exhaust and left to be squashed by a lorry in the middle of the road. "My watch, Dad, it got stolen.

Sorry I didn't tell you, I thought it'd turn up, but it looks like it's really gone," he said.

"Oh well, we'll get you another one. Don't you worry about it," said Mr Sawkins.

"Thanks, Dad!" said Ben, giving off his trademark grin.

Lily couldn't help but be amazed at how flippant someone could be at the loss of a £6,000 watch. *Oh, what it would be like to have loads of money,* she thought.

"We need to find out for sure if Mr Stoot really was the thief," said Ameshin.

"I thought you weren't interested anymore?" said Lily.

"My new violin stinks," said Ameshin. "I might as well bring a litter of kittens to the Christmas concert and teach them to squeak the notes—I'm back in."

"I'm in too. What are we going to do?" said Ben.

"Sleepover at mine, on Wednesday night. I've got a plan," said Lily.

"That's Halloween," said Ben.

"Even better," said Lily. "You'll need to bring your school uniform."

"What for?" said Ben.

"You'll find out," said Lily, followed by a wicked smile.

Chapter Nine
A Nighttime Bike Ride

A giant cake appeared from the kitchen. Lily could tell the Victoria sponge was warm. Jam was oozing out of the sides and onto the plate.

"Another cake, Mum?" said Lily.

"What's wrong, don't you like cake anymore?" said Mrs Thicke.

"That's the third cake you've baked us in two days," said Lily.

"She's just happy to have you home," said Mr Thicke.

"I'm just happy to have you home," said Mrs Thicke, as if Mr Thicke had never spoken.

"See, I knew it," said Mr Thicke. "And we're all in a better mood now all that suspension business has passed."

"That reminds me, no luck with finding your violin, Ameshin, dear?" said Mrs Thicke.

"We've given up on that, Mum. It's not worth getting into any more bother over," said Lily.

"Very wise," said Mr Thicke.

He straightened out his newspaper, signalling he agreed entirely with the sentiment of not getting into trouble.

Mrs Thicke delved a sharp knife into the cake. "Don't you girls want any then?"

"I couldn't say no. Shall I put the kettle on?" said Ameshin.

"Very polite, dear," said Mrs Thicke. "I've got a pot brewing already. Are you two doing much today?"

"We're off to the river. I'm showing Ameshin how to fish," said Lily.

The cake was scoffed down, and the girls sauntered off to the river.

Hopping off a wooden pontoon into a rowing boat, Lily helped Ameshin on board.

"Whose boat is this?" said Ameshin.

"Actually, I'm not sure," said Lily.

"How can you use it if you're not sure?"

"I've always used it," said Lily.

Ameshin smiled, shaking her head. Not in disagreement, but in pleasant surprise. She shouldn't have been surprised, Lily had this carefree way about her which still surprised Ameshin with something or other at least once a day.

Lily sliced a worm into quarters and the girls hooked them up and dangled the lines in the water.

"What now?" said Ameshin.

"Now, we wait?" said Lily.

"How long?" said Ameshin.

"Could be hours," said Lily.

"I've caught one!" Ameshin spurted in delight.

She yanked the fish out of the water and wound up her line like she'd been fishing since she was a toddler.

"Are you sodding good at everything?" said Lily, looking slightly miffed.

Ameshin shrugged, whilst the fish flapped about on the floor of the boat. Lily wrapped her hands around it, slipped it off the hook and threw it in a bucket of cold water.

"You're good at stuff, too," said Ameshin.

"Like what?" said Lily.

"Being sneaky," said Ameshin. "And being nice!"

"Nice? Well, that's great. I'm a nice, sneaky person," said Lily.

"Okay, so what have you tried to be good at?" said Ameshin.

"What do you mean?" said Lily.

"What have you applied yourself to?" said Ameshin.

Lily licked her top lip, and sucked her bottom lip in, biting it, thinking.

"I suppose, I've never applied myself to anything," said Lily.

"There you go then. Why would you be good at anything?" said Ameshin.

"I see what you mean," said Lily. "I don't deserve to be good at anything, is what you're saying."

"You have to earn your place in the world. Practice, practice, practice," said Ameshin.

"Is that what your father tells you?" said Lily.

"Word for word," said Ameshin.

"He is right though. You're so in tune with the world," said Lily.

"Well, in Japan, we say that awareness is the best gift you can give yourself," said Ameshin. "If you're aware, you're thinking all of the time about how to do things better. About how you can be better. Now, what do you want to be good at?"

"Other than being a nice sneak, you mean?"

Ameshin nodded. "I can see how much you want to fit in at school. Maybe try something that will help you do that."

"I'll have a think," said Lily.

When they got home, Mr Thicke grilled their catch-of-the-day for dinner, adding salt and a squeeze of lemon. Ameshin couldn't wait to tell her father about eating river-trout, she just had to be careful on the details. She'd be on the next flight home to Japan if he knew about her staying with the Thicke's for a week.

After the fun of the first few days of half-term, the day Ben was due to arrive was just as exciting, if not even more so. Lily took Ameshin walking in the Dorset hills. They spotted deer and collected conkers. Lily said to Ameshin she'd never be beaten at conkers when they got back to school, adding that she had quite a few tricks up her sleeve when it came to a game of conkers. Ameshin didn't have a clue what Lily had meant by a *game of conkers*. She didn't enquire, because just at that moment they reached the very top of the highest hill, with a view for miles around. Tiny churches, villages, and streams made the countryside look like a toy-play-mat. It was fair to say Ameshin fell in love with the English countryside, and even if her father did find out she'd left the school to stay with Lily for half-term, it wouldn't have mattered a drop; she wouldn't have changed the memories for the world.

Wednesday evening soon arrived, and Ben turned up moments before dinnertime. He'd brought his bicycle, a neatly rolled up sleeping bag, and a pillow, with a cricket themed print all over it.

"Don't you get fed up with cricket," said Lily.

"How could anyone get fed up with cricket?" said Ben, grinning away.

Ben's smile was infectious. He was probably the happiest seeming boy Lily had ever met, and he was a pleasure to be around.

Lily and Ameshin took Ben into Lily's room. An impressive base took up half the room, which consisted of four chairs, a few sheets, a mop-pole, to prop up the roof, and as many duvets and pillows as were going spare, which would make sleeping on the floor a lot more comfortable.

As well as den-making, after their walk, Lily and Ameshin had spent the afternoon carving frightening faces into pumpkins. Five of the orange fruits were now dotted around Lily's bedroom. Ben couldn't wait to turn the lights out later and reveal flame-lit mouths and jagged eyes, hopefully sharing a bowl of sweets and chocolates.

"I do love Halloween," said Ben. "And this is a fine den to figure out what we're going to do to solve all of these crimes."

"We won't be doing that here," said Lily. "We're going to the school, *tonight*."

It was the first Ameshin and Ben had heard of it.

"I'm not sure that's a good idea, Lily," said Ben. "Not least of all because it's the scariest night of the year, and don't you remember what happened to you two the last time you went sneaking about?"

"We need to find clues. The school is the only place we'll find them," said Lily.

"The school is the only place we'll find trouble," said Ameshin. "There's no way I'm going to an empty school in the middle of the night."

"I thought you two said you were in. Are you going to let me go on my own?" said Lily.

Ben and Ameshin looked at each other. They knew she was serious. "Okay," they said. "We're in."

The three of them enjoyed some of Mrs Thicke's beef stew, with an accompaniment of cheesy leeks and mashed potatoes. Lily had told Ben and Ameshin to eat extra food, because they had a very long night ahead of them.

Mrs Thicke had never seen three children eat so much food before. They each had three slices of bread and butter with their dinner, and an extra helping of mash.

After seeing this mass consumption of food by three young children, Mr and Mrs Thicke blessed their joint-bank-account that they only had one child to feed.

"Mum, Dad, thanks for dinner. We're going to play in the den. I've got some ghoulish tales lined up for Ben and Ameshin," said Lily. "I shan't expect you'll see us again this evening."

"Hey, Lily," said Mr Thicke. "I saw an overweight ghost the other day. I told him to get some exorcise." He chuckled away.

Lily groaned with embarrassment. She shook her head and turned to leave without responding to the joke.

"Don't scare yourselves too much, dear. And let us know if you need anything," said Mrs Thicke.

Lily, Ameshin, and Ben didn't waste a moment. As soon as they were in Lily's bedroom they got into their uniforms and climbed out of the window, sneaking three bikes quietly up the garden path.

What a rush. Being so naughty. Cycling through the darkness, seeing only what was lit up ten yards ahead. Ben felt as if he was a whole other person. He'd never done anything like this before. Ameshin worried about getting caught, but she reasoned that the school was empty, and she thought the reward of finding a clue, which could lead to finding her violin, far outweighed the risk of being caught.

Lily powered ahead on her bike, thinking of nothing but where to look first when they arrived at the school.

The roads over the Dorset hills were long and steep. Every hill seemed to drain the children's energy until they'd re-charged, freewheeling down the other side. An hour into the bike ride and the three of them were wavering.

"How much further to go?" said Ameshin.

"Just another six miles," Lily told her.

"You do realise that we're mad," said Ben. "And I still don't see why we wore our uniforms."

"Because we're going to school. You have to wear your uniform to go to school, and don't worry about feeling tired, you'll feel good when you get there, I promise," said Lily, talking through such heavy breath it sounded as if she'd almost forgotten how to speak.

"I'm not looking forward to the cycle home, put it that way," said Ameshin.

The three of them saved their breath, hardly saying another word until they'd come to a stop outside the school gates. The closed gates looked even more unwelcoming in the dead of night than they had when Lily had seen them on her first day.

"Hide the bikes in the bushes. There's a hole in the fence, just through this coppice," said Lily.

"How do you know that?" said Ben.

"I heard some sixth-formers talking about it, saying it's where they sneak out at night," said Lily.

"Sixth-formers sneak out at night? Where do they go?" said Ben.

"You really are innocent, aren't you, Ben?" said Lily.

"Well, I didn't know people broke the rules so much. It's a wonder there aren't more suspensions," said Ben.

Lily laughed. "You'll make a great prefect one day," she said.

"They might even make you the fence monitor. No one would get out of school then," said Ameshin, smirking at herself.

"All right, that's enough teasing. Are we going in, or what?" said Ben.

A short trek through the forest brought Lily's torchlight to a hole in the fence. The three of them squeezed through, stepping foot onto the school grounds.

Out the other side of the forest the night was motionless. The main house was a mass of darkness merging with a storm-grey night sky. The shadow of the abbey's tower dominated the horizon. The gravel walkway crunched beneath their feet. Even though they knew the school was empty and no one was there to hear them coming, they crept along keeping as quiet as possible.

"How are we going to get inside?" said Ben.

"We'll have to split up and check for open windows first," said Lily. "Ben, you go around to the back. Ameshin take the east side. I'll try the front and west side."

They went their separate ways. Walking from window to window, pushing upwards to see if any were open. Ben

110

and Ameshin came back around to the front, having had no luck on their sides. No luck for Lily, either.

"There's no way in," said Ben.

"There's always a way in," said Lily.

"You sound like a cat-burglar," said Ameshin.

"A cat-burglar," Lily processed that term for a moment. "That's genius, Ameshin. You've always got the answer, even if you don't know it."

Lily dashed off, where to, Ben and Ameshin had no idea, until they followed her to a back door.

"How can we get in that door? Surely, it's locked, too," said Ben.

"The cat-flap," said Lily.

Ben tilted his head, as if sizing up the cat-flap. A look of confusion brought his eyebrows closer together. "You want to get in through the cat-flap?"

"Yes," Lily smiled, letting Ben's confusion deepen for a moment longer. "I'll fetch a stick, put it through the flap, and one of you has to guide me to the key, watching through that window," said Lily.

Lily returned with a stick and got to her knees. "This should do it. If I poke it through and up to the lock, I should be able to push the key round," she said.

Both Ben and Ameshin went to the window, squashing their noses tight to the glass. They could just make out the outline of the key in the lock. Ameshin tried the torch to get a better look, but that didn't help, the light reflected back off the glass and she couldn't see anything.

111

Returning to the dim light of the night, Ameshin watched Lily's stick wobbling around the lock.

"Towards us," said Ameshin. "Can you feel it? Your stick is touching the key."

"I feel it," said Lily.

"Lower the stick and you'll find the height of the key," said Ameshin.

Lily got a good feeling for the control of the stick.

"You're right there. Push up," said Ameshin.

CLICK.

"No way," said Ben.

He jumped behind Lily, yanked the handle down and the door opened.

"There's always a way," said Lily.

Ameshin switched on her torch. "Follow me."

They crept through the kitchens, up a set of stairs and along a corridor.

A door creaked in the distance. A tapping sound moved above them.

"Did you hear that?" said Ben.

"It's a bit lively here, considering the school is empty," said Ameshin."

"Is it ever really empty?" said Lily.

"What do you mean?" said Ben.

"Haven't we told you about our game of ghost-board?" said Lily.

"No, and now doesn't seem like the right time," said Ben.

Being there in the dark and without any people around made the school house seem as if it was endless. A place of infinite corridors and mysterious doors that led to rooms which none of them had noticed before now.

"Let's start looking in rooms, shall we?" said Lily.

She twisted a door knob to enter a room that she'd never been inside of before. The door was locked. The next one was locked, too, and the next. The next door opened; another room Lily had never seen inside of. She saw a long table surrounded by chairs, and a whiteboard in the corner. *A meeting room. There'll be nothing here,* she thought.

The next room was a disused classroom, and the room opposite was the chemistry lab. All of the other rooms on the first floor were classrooms.

"Let's go to the lockers, there's nothing to find up here," said Lily.

Torchlight bounced off the walls, Ben and Ameshin followed Lily down the stairs where they passed Miss Warple's office, which was locked. They kept moving along the hallway. The oil-paintings and their haunting eyes made Lily imagine things that weren't there. She wondered if secret cameras were hidden inside of the men's eyes. Someone knew what was going on at this school, and they had to have a way of knowing. Lily hoped she was wrong about the secret cameras, but she knew something was watching them, she could feel it.

"Check all of the lockers. See if any of them are open, or loose or something," said Lily.

The three of them began pulling at locker doors. Ben was caught somewhere between feeling terrified by what he was doing, and somehow enjoying doing something he would never have imagined he would. The lockers were all securely locked.

"Let's take a look inside the caretaker's cupboard, where we found Jinny and Tom," said Lily.

They approached the first door beyond the end of the lockers. Lily twisted the handle down and pushed the door open.

It seemed that organisation was Mr Stoot's thing. Mops, buckets, brushes, nails, hammers, saws, floor-cleaning sprays, and everything was so neatly lined up, the tools of the cupboard-room looked like a squadron of the British Army standing to attention. Lily began to look through the bits and bobs.

"What exactly do you think we're looking for?" said Ben.

"Who knows," said Ameshin, pulling up a stool to reach the top shelf.

The children messed up the cupboard's military precision, knocking things over and dropping things on the floor. There was nothing to be found, but caretaker's stuff.

Lily spotted a toolbox on the floor, just underneath the bottom shelf.

Pulling it out, she opened it.

Searching through the top level, she found nothing more than screwdrivers and nails. She lifted out the top level and rummaged about the base of the box amongst screws and spanners. She saw a label. 'Attic' was written on it.

Pulling out a length of string, she said, "Maybe we're looking for this…" Lily dangled a metal key in the torchlight. "Looks like we're going up to the attic."

"I'm not sure that's a good idea," said Ben.

"Don't get scared now, Ben. Look how far we've come," said Lily, moving past him, already on her way.

Reluctantly, Ben followed the girls back along the corridor, up the stairs to the second floor and up one more flight of stairs to the attic. The attic door looked thick and heavy, made of dark wood, built to last as long as the manor house itself.

"Ameshin, would you like to try it?" said Lily, offering the key.

Ameshin took it. "I've always wanted to see what's up here," she said.

With a fiddle and a click, the door unlocked. Ameshin turned the knob, pushing the door open. Faint rays of moonlight filtered through a stained-glass window. Lily turned the torch towards the room. Orange light flitted across old boxes and trunks, and broken desks and chairs.

"It will take the rest of term to search through all of this," said Ben.

"We'd better start looking now then," said Lily.

Stepping inside, loose floorboards moved beneath their feet. Creaks filled the room with a chill.

"I have no idea how you two got me here," said Ben.

"Now that we are here, stop thinking and start looking," said Lily.

"All right, but I don't expect to find my watch up here," said Ben.

A heavy trunk with cast iron hinges was Lily's first target. She fingered the lock, one clip shot up.

The door slammed behind them.

Ben screamed louder than the girls.

Lily swished the torchlight towards the door. No one was there.

"Hello," said Lily.

Silence.

"Who's there?" said Lily.

She shifted the light to the left, lighting up a mattress on the floor. The torchlight shot across to the right-hand side of the door.

A man's face burst into the light.

He was coming closer. Lily screamed, dropping the torch. The light went out when the torch crashed to the floor. She scrambled away to go anywhere but near that man.

In the darkness, Ben, Ameshin and Lily lost each other.

The attic lights flickered on.

Lily was bottom-up inside of a wooden crate. Ameshin was hiding somewhere out of sight, and Ben was standing right in the middle of the room, still screaming, too afraid to move.

"All right. All right. That's enough screaming at this time of night. Now, when you've all calmed down, you can tell me what you're doing here," the man said.

"Mr Stoot?" said Lily, pulling herself out of the crate. "What are we doing here? What are you doing here? Is more to the point."

"*No,* considering I live up here, I think you've got the more explaining to do," said Mr Stoot.

Ameshin appeared from her hiding place. "You live up here?"

Mr Stoot didn't answer, he presumed the question was rhetorical.

"Miss Warple fired you last week," said Lily.

"I've lived up here for fifty years. Seen five Headmaster's come and go. Miss Warple doesn't know anything that goes on around here. Especially whose been stealing what," said Mr Stoot.

"Do you know who the thief is?" Lily asked.

"I know it wasn't me," said Mr Stoot.

"Miss Warple should have known too, if you've been here for fifty years—I mean why would you start stealing now, after all that time?" said Ameshin.

"I'm glad someone's got some sense. I might look a little strange to all you young-uns. But, I'm just an old man trying to make a living at a place I love," said Mr Stoot.

"I'm sorry for following you, Mr Stoot," said Lily.

He chuckled and laughed. "I was following you for most of the time, as I remember. It did give me some fun for once," he said.

"What will you do now that Miss Warple has fired you?" Ben said.

"Start stealing I suppose," Mr Stoot chuckled again.

"Is there anything you can tell us about the thefts of the violin, the watch, or the necklace?" said Lily.

"A watch has gone missing too, eh? The thief has a keen eye for something valuable, doesn't he," said Mr Stoot. He scratched away at his scarce white stubble. "I've seen those two lovebirds, Jinny and Thomas around at two of the crime scenes. Maybe that's a coincidence, I'm not blaming anyone. I've been through that myself. But, err, who knows, they could be in it together. And pretending to steal her own necklace to throw people off the scent. That wouldn't be such a bad idea."

"Two thieves?" said Ben. "That is interesting. But, we need some evidence."

"I've been all around the school looking for clues myself. I'm afraid you won't find anything. You'll have to catch the thief in the act, if it's to be proven," said Mr Stoot.

"I think we'll leave you in peace now," said Lily. "How long will you be staying up here?"

"Oh, just until the end of the week, while the school's empty. Then I'll be on my way," said Mr Stoot.

"Good luck with everything," said Lily.

"Yes, you too. Just don't go getting yourselves into any serious trouble. That Miss Warple is full of unfair discipline. Never seen anything like her," said Mr Stoot.

Ameshin and Ben wished Mr Stoot a fond farewell, and the three adventurers went on their way, no closer to solving the crimes.

The long cycle home was a tough one. On the way Lily somehow felt more confident knowing there weren't any clues she had missed somewhere around the school. She did feel for poor Mr Stoot. He had turned out to be such a kind-hearted man, and grossly misunderstood, mostly because of how he looked. *I must learn not to judge things by their looks alone,* Lily thought.

The sun was dawning back at Lily's house. Never had duvets stacked up inside a den felt so soft. The children slept until they were too hungry to sleep anymore. Ben called his father to ask if he could stay for another night. The three friends were having so much fun they didn't want it to end. Unfortunately, fun always does come to an end, and Ben went home, and Lily went back to fixing up her furniture, and Ameshin practiced on her replacement violin for the remainder of the holiday. It had been the best half-term any of them had ever had.

Chapter Ten
Quite a Find

Back inside Ben's car, the height of the Hummer made for spectacular viewing on the return to school.

"Thanks for picking us up, Mr Sawkins," said Lily.

"No trouble at all," said Mr Sawkins. "We can't have you walking to school. I can't imagine you'd ever want to go back with all that walking to do."

"The walk isn't that bad," said Lily.

She wanted to say that she would have walked fifty miles to school to come back, but actually, she didn't know if that were true herself.

Upon seeing the black gates open, Lily thought back to her dreadful first day and the events of the first half of term. So far, someone who wasn't supposed to be at the school was getting away with stealing. And Mr Stoot had lost his job, because of it. She wondered what this coming half of the term would bring in the lead up to the Christmas holidays.

What will be stolen next, I wonder? And how will I catch them?

Lily thanked Mr Sawkins again, and the three children went their separate ways to their dormitories.

Ameshin had told Lily again and again, over the past week, that she really should find something to focus on, other than solving the mystery of the missing violin, the watch, and the necklace. Lily had no idea what else she could focus on. After she'd unpacked her bags, Lily sat on her bunk and played over some options in her mind—*how about extra art on a Saturday morning, perhaps I could do that? Or join the book club, I do like to read a lot; or the chess club; or drama club—no, I don't think so; perhaps the choir? I'm sure I can sing okay.*

The dormitory door opened. A shiver moved up Lily's spine. All she could think was, *please don't be Jinny.*

"Hey, Lily. What are you up to?" said Izzy, coming into the room with more bags than a young girl should be able to carry in her arms.

Lily was relieved. "Hi, Izzy. Oh, I'm just thinking," she said.

"Anything interesting?" Izzy asked, dumping her bags on the floor.

"I need something to focus on," said Lily. "Something that keeps me out of trouble."

Izzy smiled. "You're good at trouble," she said.

"I don't mean to be. It's just a little different here to what I'm used to," said Lily.

"More strict, you mean," said Izzy.

"I'm learning how to play *the game*, put it that way," said Lily.

Izzy prepared herself to put on a deep voice, "*Life is one big game, and if you don't play it right, you won't get anywhere!* That's what my father always says. Hey, that's what you should do," said Izzy. "Play more games—didn't you tell me you were good at hockey?"

"I don't have my own stick, so I can't really play," said Lily.

Izzy unzipped a long bag. "It just so happens I have two," she pulled out a hockey stick and handed it to Lily.

Lily stared at the stick, handling it as if she'd been presented with a poisonous snake. "Thanks," she said.

"There's a pretty good set of girls this year, but with my coaching, and a lot of hard work, I reckon you could get on the team. Maybe you'll help us beat Stonemoor School one of these days," Izzy said, having not noticed the panic tumbling through Lily's eyes.

"Hockey it is then," said Lily.

She was secretly thinking to herself that hockey might have been the very last thing she would have chosen. *Why did I lie to Izzy about being okay at hockey?* She thought to herself. *I've really done it now.*

Laura and Claire came into the room, they'd been back for most of the afternoon.

"Did you hear about Jinny?" said Laura.

"No, what's that?" said Izzy.

Lily couldn't care less.

"She's quite ill," said Claire. "And her parents don't want her back at school for at least another week."

Lily felt bad about not caring after hearing the news. She didn't wish being ill on her. "What's wrong with her?" she said.

"Glandular fever they think," said Claire.

"The kissing disease," said Laura.

"There's no such thing as *the kissing disease*!" said Izzy.

"Yes there is, and Jinny's got it," said Laura.

"Well, who has she been kissing so much as to get something called *the kissing disease?*" said Izzy.

Lily knew. She wondered who else did.

"Nobody's sure. You don't always get glandular fever from kissing, but we reckon she's been up to something with somebody," said Laura.

There was Lily's answer. No one else knew Jinny had been sneaking around with Tom Allen, except for Ben, Ameshin, and Mr Stoot. The photograph they had of Jinny and Tom was a great bargaining tool, she knew it. In the meantime, another week without Jinny was going to be bliss.

"We should make her a get-well card," said Lily.

"What a bright idea," said Claire. "I've got art tomorrow. I'll make it then."

The girls carried on chatting about their week, and the atmosphere in the dorm was somehow a lot more playful without Jinny around. The lights went out and eventually the talking died down after they said their goodnight's. Lily was beginning to feel right at home at her new school. *I do like it here,* she thought to herself, *even more so without Jinny.*

*

Mr Ballard walked into the English room. A gaggle of chairs were sent sliding back across the wooden floor, knocked by the backs of legs as the children stood to welcome their teacher into the room.

"Everybody sit," said Mr Ballard.

Lily came running in. She couldn't believe Mr Ballard had beaten her to the classroom.

"Sorry, sir," said Lily. She took a seat beside Ameshin.

Mr Ballard was aware the two of them were not supposed to be sitting together, but he thought perhaps that punishment was over by now. "Where have you been, Lily?" he said.

"I nearly forgot to bring my conkers for break time, sir," she said.

"Lily, I hate to tell you this, conkers is not a game that is allowed at this school," said Mr Ballard.

"No conkers? Are you sure? It's so much fun, sir, and it's only for one week of the year," said Lily. "At Stakdale everybody played conkers."

"This is not Stakdale. And, yes, I *am* sure that conkers are not allowed. I would ask you not to question your superiors. If you're feeling brave take it up with Miss Warple, should you not agree with me," said Mr Ballard.

He flicked his fingers a few times towards himself, meaning for Lily to bring the conkers forward.

"Yes, sir," said Lily, dragging her feet across the floor to hand over her prizewinning conkers. When she gave them to Mr Ballard he turned his hand over and dropped them into a metal bin with a loud clang. She wished she hadn't gone and got them in such a hurry now.

"Did you all write your poetic love letters from Romeo to Juliet?" Mr Ballard said.

"Yes, sir," the class returned.

"Lily, collect up the letters before you sit back down," said Mr Ballard.

It was not the start to the week Lily was hoping for. She hated some rules, or rather she didn't understand them. She stared at the bin all lesson, wishing she could have her conkers back. Wishing she was still at Stakdale, just for a day or two. If she were there, come break-time, the bell would sound and a good hundred or so children would flood out to the playground to see if their conker-on-a-string could defeat the biggest and best of them. The conker rules at Stakdale were simple. The last remaining whole conker in the school was crowned the winner, and Mr Ballard had just thrown a potential champion conker into the bin, without an ounce of respect for it.

The no-conker-rule made Lily mad at such a fun thing being looked upon with such wickedness. *I think it's time everyone loosened up a bit around here,* she thought to herself.

After a lesson of not listening to a word on why Romeo and Juliet was one of the greatest love stories of all time, the bell sounded. Ameshin ran off to practice, and Lily watched everyone sprinting across to the tuck shop, which was inside of the tea rooms. The line coming out of the shop was incredible. The whole school rushed to buy sweets and crisps to snack on over the twenty-minute break.

The whole school that was, except for Lily.

Lily then noticed something. Robert Groom didn't go to the tuck shop either. He sat down by himself looking a little lonely. Lily had half a mind to go and tick him off for telling people about how poor she was. He'd started all sorts of rumours that people like Jinny were using to poke fun at her. *Just because my father doesn't earn as much as his does, that doesn't give him the right to gossip about it,* she thought. It was a shame too, because they had unexpectedly gotten along very well on the river trip, but Lily had decided she wasn't going to speak to him any longer. He had his chance to make it up to her for being a shrub on the first day of school, and he had thrown it back in her face.

Lily left the school to their snacks and trundled back inside to peek through the window of the English classroom. She wanted her conkers back, but Mr Ballard was at the desk, marking papers.

I can't let this week go by without playing conkers, Lily thought. *I know what I can do.*

Lunchtime soon came around. Lily decided time was too precious to be sitting around eating. While everyone was in the food hall, Lily took a stroll past the grounds of the abbey. She walked all the way to the end of the golf course and headed into the woodlands that surrounded the school. The woods were out of bounds, and she knew it. She also knew a discredit would befall her if she was caught, but for what she had in mind she thought it was well worth getting a discredit.

In the woods, Lily crunched over twigs and kicked through fallen leaves, keeping her head tilted up skywards as she walked along. She was looking up to see what kind of trees she was passing. There were thousands of silver birch, the odd, giant oak tree, and plenty of beech and ash, but there were no signs of any conker trees.

Lily found herself in the middle of the woods. It was dark and quiet. The only sound was the banging of a woodpecker's beak in the distance, and the shuffling paws of squirrels collecting nuts from amongst the leaves. She was about to give up on her conker search and go back to school when, in the distance, she saw a break of light coming through the trees. She moved towards the light, and the closer she came the more Lily thought she could see the distinctive leaves of a conker tree.

Lily's walk quickened.

She started to run.

Bursting into an opening in the forest, Lily laid eyes on the finest and most untouched collection of conkers anyone had ever discovered. They were everywhere. Large conkers; double conkers; triple conkers; conkers still wrapped in their shells.

Lily held open her school bag and began to pick up the biggest and best of them from the forest floor. At Lily's old school she could have sold some of these conkers for a pound each, most of the others for 20p. *I can probably get double the prices at this school,* she thought. The idea of having lots of money led her to another idea. *If I had lots of money, I could leave it lying about for the thief, and trick him into taking it.* Lily's mind ticked over with thief-catching ideas as she collected the conkers.

Recently, she'd started to worry that herself, Ben, and Ameshin were getting no closer to solving the ghost's answer. She now knew that catching *the one who shouldn't be there* would take something clever, something unobvious, and something the whole school would take an interest in. Lily had everything planned by the time she had loaded her bag with conkers.

One final search remained. Lily set about finding her champion conker. It didn't take long. She lined up seven green spiked balls that she'd earmarked as champion level contenders.

She cracked open the shells.

There was nothing worthy.

These conkers were sloppy slugs. She needed armoured snails.

She looked up, almost praying to the sky. And in all its divine glory, she caught sight of a golden-delicious-sized conker shell clinging on for the last days of autumn.

Scavenging through the leaves for a suitable stick, Lily pulled one up which was just the right weight.

She aimed; she threw; she watched the stick bash into the conker and drop; hit a branch, and split the shell three ways.

The conker dropped at her feet.

She peeled off the remaining fresh shell. Never before had she seen a conker so magnificent, so strong, and so sparklingly proud.

"This is going to be brilliant," she said to herself.

Chapter Eleven
The Wrong Winner

Following Thursday's assembly, where the only thing of note was a reminder of fireworks night being held the next evening, the children meandered along to their first class of the day.

Lily and Ameshin settled into their seats in the maths room, not having to worry any longer about being separated. It seemed the teachers had forgotten about that punishment.

Lily lifted the lid of her desk, fishing out a conker on a string. "Hey look, Amie, a conker. See if there's one in your desk," she said.

Ameshin opened up her desk. There she saw a beautiful shiny conker. She took it out and wondered what conkers were doing in their desks.

Lily turned to the desk behind, where Ben was sitting. "Hey, Ben, look what was inside of mine and Ameshin's desks," she said. "Is there one in yours?"

Ben's face lit up when he saw a conker inside of his desk, too. "Hey everyone, me, Ameshin, and Lily had a conker in our desks."

The rest of the class lifted up their desk lids in a frantic hurry. To everyone's surprise there was a conker on a string sitting inside of every desk. The class started chattering as to how this could have happened, questioning who would have been brave enough to do it, saying how they couldn't wait to get outside and have a secret game of conkers at break time.

"Won't we get into trouble if we get caught?" said Georgina.

"We can't all get in trouble, can we?" said Lily. "What can they do if all of us are playing conkers?"

"I suppose you're right," said Georgina.

"I'd hide them away until break time though," said Lily.

Mr Woodcock walked into the room. The class stuffed their conkers into their pockets as they stood up. The lesson went on as usual, except for a few conker challenges being set-up via notes passed around the classroom. The bell rang and the upper third class hurried out onto the playing fields. For once the tuck shop queue was nearly empty.

It soon transpired it was not only the upper third class who had found conkers hidden in their desks, but every year up to the sixth formers were talking about a *Conker Miracle* at Winkton Abbey.

Lily chuckled to herself when she heard no one in the Upper Fourth B class had opened a single desk during their lesson. When they heard about the other conkers, the entire class hurried back to the classroom to get theirs.

Lily's plan was working perfectly.

A few prefects confiscated conkers, and word soon reached Miss Warple that somehow every pupil in the school had gotten hold of a conker. Little did Lily know it, but some of the other pupils had already been secretly playing conkers all along. They were much more open about it now the prefects couldn't keep up with the conker epidemic.

The buying and selling of conkers became a rife trade throughout the school. Lily was ever so pleased with herself, but she knew that what she had planned to come was going to be even better.

She only needed the right sort of help for everything to work.

*

The evening of the school fireworks display meant a shortened prep. In the cold and dark of the early winter evening, boarders and day-pupils began to collect outside on the sports fields, ready to watch fireworks and the burning of a gigantic bonfire.

While the excitement of a raging fire, and twizzling fireworks was going on, Lily, Ameshin, and Ben went to find Thomas Allen. Predictably, they found him right at the back of the crowd. He was watching the fireworks with his girlfriend and his friends. Lily was suitably amused when she saw a couple of the head boy's friends playing conkers.

She went up to Tom, alone. "Can I have a word, please, Tom?" she said.

"Hello, Thicke," said Tom, sounding curious. A firework screamed into the sky, everyone watched. "What is it?" he asked.

"In private would be better," said Lily. She turned and walked back towards Ben and Ameshin.

Tom followed after her. "Can't you go to your House Captain for whatever it is?" he said.

"Not really. It's about you and Jinny," said Lily.

Tom's eyes exploded with panic. He saw Ben and Ameshin giving him a judging kind of look, for sneaking around with another girl. "Jinny who?" he said.

"Jinny Green. And there's no point in pretending. I know all about it," said Lily.

"I really don't know what you're talking about," said Tom.

Ameshin passed Lily a photograph. "Perhaps this will help you remember?" she said, handing him the photograph. A firework flashed red in the sky, helping to light up the incriminating photograph.

"You know Jinny is quite ill from all of your kissing, don't you? She's off next week, as well as last week," said Lily.

"All right, Thicke, what do you want?" said Tom.

"The whole school has been given one conker each. I found them all in the woods the other day, and I pierced and strung every one of them. Then I got out of bed, two nights ago and hid nearly three-hundred conkers in all of the desks around the school," said Lily.

"It was you?" said Tom. "You could get expelled for that."

"I don't think so. I have the head boy on my side to make sure that doesn't happen. Here's what I need from you," said Lily, keeping a confident stance. "You and your friends will arrange a conker competition, played under your supervision, and with safety rules in place so Miss Warple has no objections. To enter the competition will cost £2.00. Perhaps don't mention that part to Miss Warple, it's up to you. The winner will take home around £500. That's all I want you to do, *for now*."

Tom stared at the brave third year girl in front of him, never imagining he would be blackmailed into doing anything like this by someone who was so small, and who looked so innocent beneath a woolly hat.

"What's in this for you?" said Tom.

"I get to play conkers," said Lily. "And I get to have a chance at catching our thief when I win the money."

"Miss Warple has made it clear Mr Stoot was the thief," said Tom.

"I'm afraid that's not the truth of the matter. The thief is still in this school," said Lily. "In fact, Mr Stoot named you as one of his main suspects."

"Me? That's ridiculous," said Tom.

"I don't think it's you, Tom, but if I can win the £500, I think I'll have what I need to catch our thief," said Lily.

"You're a smart girl, Lily. You'd do well staying out of trouble. But, I can see you care about your friends enough to help them this much. I'll arrange the competition," said Tom.

"Enjoy the rest of the fireworks," said Lily. "Miss Warple is standing at the front, near the bonfire. I'd suggest tonight's a good time to ask her. She's on her fifth glass of mulled wine."

Lily kept a close eye on Tom. After a while he went over to Miss Warple, who was being louder than her usual loud-self.

Tom requested the conker competition.

"Of course, you can, Mr Allen!" Miss Warple sputtered. "Two pounds to enter? I might enter myself!"

"Thank you, Miss Warple," said Tom.

"A sports-day for conkers. I think it's a wonderful idea," said Miss Warple. "Cancel prep on Tuesday evening for the final. The competition will be held in the lunch-hall, the first round starts at breaktime."

Lily wished that Miss Warple was this pleasant to everyone.

*

No sooner had the break-bell rung on Tuesday, when everyone rushed to the year-group noticeboards. On an A4 sheet, headed "Winkton Abbey Conker Championship" Tom had arranged league games for the year groups and the teachers. The notes explained that the winner's name from each round was to be placed into a hat and randomly selected to play their next opponent. Lily and Tom had finalised the rules over the weekend, and the only things entrants were not allowed to do were swing sideways, or upwards.

Rain was pouring down outside. The perfect weather for a conker competition in the food hall.

Scampering through the school corridors, every method of hardening a conker shell was being discussed. The children talked about how they'd soaked their conkers in vinegar; and painted them in varnish; and used the home economics ovens to bake them for an hour to harden them up.

Having run from the geography room, Lily and Ameshin were the first to arrive at the noticeboard for the third years. Ameshin didn't often skip violin practice, but as soon as Lily had told her the plan to catch the thief, and that she had been the one to put the conkers in the desks, Ameshin didn't want to miss one second of the competition.

Reading through the board, Ameshin said, "Lily, you're playing Robert Groom."

"Good," said Lily. "You've got Harry Summers."

Ben wasn't smiling for once. "I've got Georgina, the blooming class genius. I hate losing to girls," he said.

Tom shouted out, "Can I have your attention please?"

The children in the food hall calmed to listen to the head boy. "We have marked out with a cross on the floor where each opponent shall stand. You can see marked on the wall where your year group is due to do battle. George, Emily, Kate, Andrew, and Stephen are the five prefects umpiring your games. If there are any disputes my say will be final. The prize will be £500 for the winner, and the rest of the prize money will go towards books for the school. We should have about 350 entrants if the staff join in. Not only that, but Miss Warple has said the winner will receive three credits towards the Winkton Abbey Cup."

The school cheered. Each one of them hoping they would be the one to win £500 and three credits for their house.

"Boys and girls, teachers and staff, good luck to everyone. Let the games begin," said Tom.

The food hall became a metropolis of excitement.

The prefect-umpires announced each game as the first matches got underway. Ameshin vs Harry was first up for the third years. Emily, Izzy's older sister, was the umpire for the third-year games. She collected £2.00 each from Ameshin and Harry, before they took their positions.

Ameshin had never swung a conker in her life. Standing in front of everyone, about to do so, she felt a wrench turning her stomach.

Emily tossed a coin. Ameshin called heads. Heads it was.

"Ameshin to go first," said Emily.

Ameshin studied the subtle sway of Harry's conker. The crowd watched with keen eyes, waiting for her to move.

Ameshin wrapped the string around her index finger, her other hand stretched the conker out, as if aiming with a bow and arrow. In one smooth move she swung her conker down, around and around, out wide, and whipped it back in with a downward karate-like chop. Lily had never seen anything like it. Ameshin's conker smacked into Harry's and the poor boy's nut shattered into twenty pieces. He was left holding a sorry looking piece of string, and a rather shocked look on his face. Ameshin was the first through to the next round, and she had thoroughly enjoyed her first game of conkers. Even though it hadn't lasted more than one swing.

"Robert Groom versus Lily Thicke," Emily called out.

"Here's my two pounds," said Lily.

Everyone waited for Robert to come forward, especially Lily who still owed him one for shouting his mouth off about her parents being poor.

Robert didn't come forward. He stayed standing at the back of crowd. "I don't want to play conkers," he said.

"Come on, Robert, it's only a bit of fun. You do have a conker, don't you?" said Lily.

Robert held out a fine looking conker. Lily thought it looked like a winner to her.

"I'm not paying to enter something I probably won't win," he said.

"In that case, Lily goes through to the next round to play Ameshin," Emily said.

"Wait," said Lily. "Robert why don't you want to play?"

"I'm not going to play and that's that," said Robert. He threw his conker on the floor and ran out of the lunch room.

Lily didn't mind too much at getting a bye into the second round, but now she had to wait to have her first game, and that was against Ameshin. Of course, it didn't matter if either of them won and went on to win the main prize, but Lily had planned to win the money herself in order to catch the thief. Thinking ahead to if that all worked out, she could then give the recovered prizemoney to her parents.

Lily wandered up and down the year groups, observing techniques and weaknesses. After watching most of the games she noted the best of the players were Roger Jenkins, the top cricketer in the school, from the fifth year; Virginia Hank, the deputy head girl; Mr Tate, the history teacher; Miss Warple looked worryingly good; Izzy was excellent; and there were quite a few more contenders Lily thought might put up a good fight on her way to winning.

The first round of games drew to a close and the bell rang.

Tom shouted across the food hall, "Back here at lunchtime, everyone please, for the following rounds."

The school disappeared to their classes, telling tales of smashing up conkers and exaggerating their own victories.

One hour later and the school was promptly rushing back inside the food hall. The teachers wondered why the lessons hadn't been cancelled for the hour in between break and lunch, none of the students had been paying attention anyway, they had all turned conker mad.

The children weren't much interested in lunch. Mrs Plumley sat in a corner with a sour face on, when no one touched the shepherd's pie she'd made for lunch. At least the apple crumble went down a treat for those students watching the second round.

Emily announced, "Ameshin Chi versus Lily Thicke,"

Ameshin and Lily stepped forward.

"I don't mind stepping down," Ameshin whispered.

"Don't be silly. The best conker will win anyway, so we might as well test each other's," said Lily.

"Heads or tails?" Emily said, catching the coin in mid-air, flipping it onto the back of her hand.

"Heads," said Lily.

"Ameshin to go first," said Emily.

"Are you sure about this?" said Ameshin.

"Just hit me," said Lily.

Ameshin's eyes tensed up, watching Lily's conker. The same as she'd done before, Ameshin held her conker out tight like an arrow poised on a bow-string, her face washed with a focus that seemed to go beyond human senses. She swung her conker down, up, out high and wide and whipped it back in with a downward pull. Her conker smacked into Lily's. Lily grimaced as her string yanked hard at her finger. Opening one eye, Lily saw that her conker was still whole.

"What do I do now?" said Ameshin.

"I hit yours," said Lily.

Lily didn't do anything fancy with her first strike. She wanted to get her aim feeling good before she tried riskier shots. Lily's and Ameshin's game went on for a good five minutes. It soon became clear they both had rock solid conkers. All of the other second and third round games, and some of the fourth and fifth rounds had finished, and Lily and Ameshin were still going.

Ameshin took a swing and completely missed Lily's conker. She hadn't focused enough and rushed her shot.

"Two free shots," Emily said, after Ameshin had missed.

Ameshin had no idea those were the rules. She steadied her conker in mid-air. Lily raised her conker high and released it with a smashing follow through that swung her conker back into her hand, without hesitation she attacked using the slingshot momentum of the first swing.

Ameshin's conker exploded.

Both of them smiled and shook hands. Those watching, and that was quite a few by now, started to say

Lily might win the whole competition after what they'd just seen.

Lily beat Izzy. Then she beat Georgina. She was in the semi-finals against Roger Jenkins. The other semi-finalists were Miss Warple and Peter Harman. Peter was a thick-set boy, strong and stocky. *No-one in their right mind would want to play Miss Warple in the final,* thought Lily, *but I wouldn't want to play Peter either.*

The end-of-lunch bell went.

Tom stood on a bench to get everyone's attention. "All right, the excitement is over until we meet again later at 16:30," he said.

Lily and Ameshin trotted along for a double lesson of PE. They were out on the field in double quick time, and Lily even remembered to bring her hockey stick.

Mrs Williams sorted the third years into two groups; those who were trying for sports teams; and those who were not.

"Have fun running around the field," Lily said to Ameshin.

"Have fun pretending you can play hockey," said Ameshin, jogging off with a laugh.

Lily was not looking forward to it. Last week, after she'd agreed with Izzy that she would play hockey, she hadn't realised that just by holding a stick in her hand it meant she was automatically trying out for the school team.

Mrs Williams had almost laughed out loud when she saw Lily trying to run and control the ball with a stick at the same time. It might have been funny had it not hurt Lily so much every time she fell over her own stick. Lily was determined to do better this week, and her confidence was high after winning a few games of conkers.

"Do you think you can win the conker competition?" Izzy said, as they warmed up in the rain.

"I don't want to play against Miss Warple, but if I do, yes, I think I can win," said Lily.

"None of us can believe Miss Warple let everyone play conkers. It's unheard of, so my sister says," said Izzy. "More important things though, let's get you fit to play hockey for the school. I think we've got dribbling drills today."

Izzy, Lily, and the hockey girls from the third year, wore themselves out with Mr Waterman's hockey drills for the next two hours. Considering Lily must have had plenty on her mind, by the end of practice she thought she didn't do half bad—at least she hadn't fallen over.

Fresh out of the shower, Lily was the first back in the food hall. She went across to read the noticeboards. Completed games had been crossed through and she noticed the games had been timed. Miss Warple had won every single one of her games in under two minutes. Lily and Ameshin's game had lasted for fifteen minutes. Lily just hoped that her conker hadn't been weakened too much in all of that time.

The food hall began to fill back up, with everyone having finished school for the day. Miss Warple marched into the room. She had eyes only for Peter Harman, her next opponent.

Tom stood up to get the games back under way. "Can I please have Lily Thicke, Roger Jenkins, Peter Harman, and Miss Warple to their places," he said.

The school cheered and clapped, some stomped their feet and drummed on the tables with their hands.

Lily stood opposite Roger. Peter stood opposite Miss Warple. Tom threw a coin in the air, holding it tight to the back of his hand. "Ladies call," he said.

"Heads," said Lily and Miss Warple at the same time.

He removed his hand from above the coin. "The boys to go first," said Tom.

The boys took their positions, stepping one foot forward, ready to strike. Cheers and jeers and the smell of roast beef wafting from Mrs Plumley's kitchen added to the entertainment.

Roger swung at Lily's conker. The might of the swing sent a crack echoing through the lunch hall. Lily couldn't see a crack in her conker. A wry smile broke through when she realised Roger's conker had been damaged.

"Varnish doesn't work as well as they say it does," said Lily.

Roger dangled his injured nut. Lily pulled her conker down through the air with as much force as she could muster. Roger's conker split into two and fell to the floor.

The school cheered for Lily. Ben and Ameshin stepped in to congratulate her.

"That was lucky," Lily said to Ameshin. "I wouldn't have stood a chance in the final if my conker had another long game."

They turned their attention to the other semi-final.

Peter was a bag of nerves playing against Miss Warple. That stare she gave the children was putting him on edge. He swung and missed, and Miss Warple's first shot knocked Peter's conker off the string and on to the floor.

"Stampsys!" Miss Warple cried. She raised her foot and squashed Peter's conker like a bug.

Half of the room didn't know if that was allowed, but it was soon agreed upon that she was well within her right to stamp on Peter's conker after shouting 'stampsys'.

Miss Warple whooped. Celebrating with far too much cockiness for anyone else to be happy for her.

Once again, the whole school had its eyes on Lily Thicke. They were willing for her to step forward and beat Miss Warple in the final. Willing for her not to be nervous, but none of them could chant her name or call for her to win, because Miss Warple would make a note of who wanted her to lose.

Tom announced the last match. "The final, boys and girls. Playing for a jackpot of £500, and three house credits. Can I have Miss Warple and Lily Thicke to your places," he said.

Lily walked over to take her spot. She felt as if she was floating along like a dandelion in the wind, she could hardly feel her legs touching the ground. Miss Warple strode to her spot, confidence oozed. They stood opposite each other. Lily was four feet tall with broken glasses and a worried face. Miss Warple was six foot, three inches, staring down at Lily's head beneath her, with no other thoughts on her mind but crushing.

"I call heads," said Miss Warple.

Tom hadn't asked her. He flipped the coin anyway. "Miss Warple to begin," he said.

Silence fell across the room. People didn't want to cheer, and they didn't want to boo.

Miss Warple stood to attack. She released a full swing from high above Lily's static conker which knocked her nut swinging wildly into a round-the-world loop.

"A full-loop hit," said Tom. "Miss Warple to go again."

The next strike came quick. Miss Warple lashed her conker through the air. Her aim was off and the strings tangled and twisted.

"Strings!" Miss Warple shouted. "That's my go again!"

She made another big hit on Lily's conker and this game was turning into a bloodbath.

Lily finally had her first go. In her mind she went over everything she could do to win. Tactics were difficult because she'd never played someone so tall before. She was almost swinging upwards in order to hit Miss Warple's conker. She aimed. She poised for attack. She fired and the strings tangled again.

"Strings," Lily shouted.

The look in Miss Warple's eyes could have knocked an elephant off its feet. She pulled her string sharply down. Lily's string was pulled out of her hand and her conker fell to the floor.

"Stampsys!" Miss Warple cried, her eyes alive with menace. She squashed Lily's conker and threw her arms into the air, cheering for herself.

Lily looked up at Tom with questioning eyes, hoping he would call foul play.

"The winner is, Miss Warple," he said, holding out a giant wedge of cash to her, which had all been put into notes.

Miss Warple snatched the money. Lily's chin dropped to her chest. Her plan to catch the thief was ruined.

Counting the money, Miss Warple said, "I think we can all agree the best player won here today. And oh, look at that, there's still time for some prep before dinner. Back to work everyone," she barked. "I will be keeping my winnings on my desk for a reminder to you all that one day you might become as good as me at doing things. And all three of the credits will go to Drake house. First place always deserves more reward than those lacking behind."

Miss Warple skipped out of the room and the school begrudgingly sat down to get on with some work.

"Sorry, Lily, that wasn't fair," someone from Drake house said to her as they passed by.

A few more *sorry's* came her way, but Lily now didn't feel hard done by at all, in fact she was quite happy, and she was smiling.

"What are you smiling for?" said Ameshin.

"Miss Warple just did my job for me," said Lily. "She told the entire school the £500 would be sitting on her desk. All we need to do to catch our thief is keep a very close eye on her office."

Chapter Twelve
The Wrong Blazer

Lily saw Ben standing in a doorway nearby to Miss Warple's office. Nothing unusual about that, except it was 02:00am and Ben looked as if he was asleep.

"Pssst," said Lily.

Ben's eyes shot open.

"Is my turn over already?" said Ben. "That felt quick tonight."

"Probably because you were asleep," said Lily.

"How long are we going to keep this up for? I'm really tired," said Ben.

"I know, but it'll be worth it. You do want your watch back, right?" said Lily.

"I do, but I want some sleep as well," said Ben.

"It looked like you were getting plenty of sleep to me," said Lily. "I take it you didn't see anyone?"

"Sorry," said Ben, not knowing where to look for the feeling of embarrassment. "I didn't see anyone, no."

"We need to catch them," said Lily. "What if they steal something more important than Ameshin's violin, or your watch, or Jinny's necklace?" said Lily.

"I know, but what if the thief isn't interested in this money? We've been doing this for a week now," said Ben.

"I haven't heard of many thief's who aren't interested in money," said Lily.

"We could get in a lot of trouble for this," said Ben.

"Remember, if someone catches you, act like you're sleep-walking," said Lily. "I don't think you'll find that too hard."

Ben grinned. "Good night, Lily," he said.

"I hope you get some sleep," said Lily.

Ben went on his way, leaving Lily on look-out duty.

With nothing much to think about in the darkness, Lily leant up against the doorframe thinking about Jinny. She had returned to school looking rather frail after her illness. Lily surmised that nothing had been stolen since Jinny was absent and she could well have made up her necklace being stolen to throw everyone off the scent, like Mr Stoot had said. Other than that, Lily had no other theories on who else could be involved. The thief was a ghost themselves. Lily toyed with the idea that a poltergeist was playing games with them, since they had been playing games with the ghost-board. The mystery was a constant nagging on Lily's mind. She felt she wouldn't be able to rest until she had solved what was going on.

Lily had the last watch of the night and when the sun came up, she was the only one eating breakfast in the lunch hall, when Ameshin walked in.

"You look good in that," said Ameshin.

Lily looked down at her hockey skort, and tight long socks. "Do I?" she said.

"It's better than what the choir wear," said Ameshin, letting loose a smile.

"This is all your fault, you know," said Lily. "If you didn't leave me for hours on end, I wouldn't have to play hockey."

"What's my fault? That you're fitter, healthier, and looking better now, than when I first met you?" said Ameshin.

"You know what I mean. It's embarrassing not being as good as the others. And before you say it, I know, practice makes perfect," said Lily.

"If you're not as good as you want to be, you have to play more," said Ameshin.

"I play on Mondays, Wednesdays, and Saturdays. And sometimes Izzy and I have a knock about at break times. I can't play any more than that," said Lily.

"I practice violin up to four hours a day, every day, and that's why I'll be able to play for my country. Because I worked the hardest," said Ameshin.

"I can't believe we haven't got your violin back yet. Do you miss it?" said Lily.

A sadness glazed over Ameshin's eyes. "My violin wasn't just a part of me, it was a part of where I come from. It was the heart of my family, the heart of Japanese music in a way. I wish every day that it would come back to me," she said.

"You have to believe it will. I won't stop trying for you," said Lily.

"HURRY UP, LIL!" Izzy shouted from across the room.

"Looks like I've got to go. Have a good practice," said Lily, as she ran to join Izzy.

"Don't fall over your stick," Ameshin called after her.

Lily arrived for Saturday morning hockey training right on time. The girls were starting off with a lap around the pitch, and for the first time ever, Lily found herself experiencing a strange feeling. She found that she could compete with the fitter girls, who had always been much quicker at running than she had. She pushed herself harder, upping her speed around the corners of the pitch. She was always the last to finish the warm up lap, but not today. Lily finished her lap at the same time as some of the quicker girls. *I am getting fitter,* she thought to herself.

"It's time we figured out what position to get you into," said Izzy. "You've got a horrid shot on you, and your dribbling needs a lot of work. Play in defence today, will you?"

"Sure, I'll try," said Lily.

But Lily didn't just try. She gave it everything she had. She found that she had a talent for reading where the ball was going to be passed to next. She could spot the spaces attackers were going to run to, and when they were going to shoot or fake a shot. Lily hounded down, and blocked runs, and blocked shots. By the end of the session, Lily's team had won 6-1, and the hockey team manager, Mr Waterman, had said he was very impressed with Lily's defending.

In the changing rooms, after practice, Izzy was going on about how much better Lily had become at hockey. "At first I thought there was no hope for you, but we'll make a player of you yet," she said.

Lily smiled and went to grab her blazer. It wasn't on the hook where she'd left it.

"Hey, has anyone seen my blazer?" said Lily.

The girls looked about for a spare blazer.

"Oh, sorry, Lily," said a girl, called Jessica. "Does your blazer have someone else's name in it? A Jessica Park?"

"Yes, that's the one," Lily looked embarrassed. "It's second-hand, you see. Honestly, I didn't think I'd like it at this school, so I never bothered to stitch in my own name badge."

"Sorry, here you go," said Jessica, handing back Lily's blazer.

"That's okay, the same thing happened to a friend of mine earlier in the term," said Lily.

Something clicked in Lily's mind.

Lily's mouth and whole face changed somehow.

"Are you okay?" said Jessica. "Do you still not like it at the school?"

Lily found herself in a daze. "No, I really love the school. I hope I'll be here forever. I've got to go, sorry, I've just had a thought," she said.

Lily ran out of the changing rooms and hurried over to the art room, where she knew Ben would be on a Saturday morning.

"Ben, follow me," said Lily.

He had his face right up close to a painting of a cricket scene he was working on, delicately brushing red onto a tiny ball. "Just one second," he said.

Lily yanked him up by the arm. He dropped his brush with a yelp. "There's no time to waste," she said.

After being pulled along for a few yards he ran after her, asking what was going on. Lily said nothing as they bolted down corridors to reach the music room for Ameshin.

"I'm calling an emergency meeting. Come on," said Lily.

The three of them marched outside into the sunshine, pacing across the cricket pitch.

"One, two, three, sit," said Lily.

They sat on the spot.

"What is it, Lily? This had better be important," said Ameshin, concerned she was missing her practice.

"Oh, it's important all right. I know who the thief is," said Lily.

"How?" said Ben.

"It's been staring me in the face all this time," said Lily.

"Well who is it?" said Ben.

"The thief is Robert Groom," said Lily.

"Why do you think that?" said Ameshin.

"Think about it. Ben, what was the name inside of his blazer when you took it by accident?" said Lily.

"Benjamin Reeves, I think it was," said Ben.

"Why would someone as rich as Robert have a second-hand blazer?" said Lily.

"That's no proof," said Ameshin.

"No, but when we went to the river, Robert had no wellies, and he had holes in his shoes. He showed me himself," said Lily.

"That doesn't mean he's a thief though," said Ben.

"A taxi came to pick him up when he went home at half-term, yet he turned up on the first day of term in a Rolls Royce, with a chauffeur," said Lily.

"What if his dad couldn't make it to pick him up? I don't see your point," said Ameshin.

"Robert is the only one here, as well as me, who doesn't buy sweets from the tuck shop at lunchtime. He was the only one who wouldn't pay the £2.00 fee to enter the conker competition. He has holes in his shoes and wears an old-boy's blazer. Robert Groom is poorer than I am, and there is a reason that he shouldn't be here, just like the ghost said," said Lily, crossing her arms in victory.

"That does all sound very strange when you put it all together," said Ben.

"I thought he was all right when we spent the day together by the river, but then he started to spread it about that my parents didn't have any money. He's a dirty goat-hoof if you ask me," said Lily.

"He must have spread those rumours to help fool the others into thinking he's rich. We still need to catch him out though," said Ameshin.

"We will. I'll be watching him everywhere he goes," said Lily.

Chapter Thirteen
Bad Luck

Robert was easy to keep an eye on. He didn't have any friends, he didn't have any hobbies, and he was punctual for every single lesson.

After Robert-watching for a few days, and in the knowledge that Miss Warple hardly ever left her office, except for assemblies, Lily deduced the only time Robert would be able to get away with stealing the five-hundred pounds would be at night.

As it happened, one of Tom's good friends, a prefect called James Shawe, was in the same dorm as Robert. Tom promised Lily that James would keep an eye on Robert at all times, whenever they wouldn't be able to. If Robert snuck out at night, James would see him and follow; if he said anything strange, or acted peculiarly, James would let Tom know.

Lily made Tom promise that the next time something was stolen, he would have eyes all over Robert to catch him with the goods. Lily was sure they would catch him.

The boy that wasn't supposed to be at Winkton Abbey, surely wouldn't be for much longer.

It was all very exciting, knowing they might soon catch the thief. Lily was lying awake in her bed not being able to stop thinking. She was sure Robert was going to steal the five-hundred pounds.

Perhaps I should make friends with him, she thought.

Jinny's snorty snoring, which had gotten worse since she'd been ill, disturbed Lily's train of thought. She started thinking whether, or not, Jinny coming back to school was a good thing. It seemed the better she got, the worse she got, and Jinny was nearly back to her old self, winding people up like she always had. Lily wondered what made Jinny do it. She had glimpses of showing that she had a kind side, but then she'd insult someone and laugh at them. It was hard to like anyone who was up and down like that all of the time.

One more snore and that's enough for me, Lily said to herself.

Jinny snorted and knowing she wasn't going to get any sleep for a while, Lily got out of bed. She threw an extra jumper over her pyjama top, grabbed her torch, and crept out of the dorm.

The hallway was dark, but for the coloured light of the stained glass windows shining against the wall in the moonlight. She didn't have a plan as to where to go, she just wanted a wander. On tip-toes she padded silently down the stairs. Walking out in the halls in the dark reminded her of sneaking about with Ben and Ameshin at Halloween. She hoped Mr Stoot wouldn't jump out on her again. She knew it would be unlikely, she'd seen the old caretaker leaving shortly after half-term.

I hope he can have his job back once this is sorted out, she thought.

Lily wandered into the food hall. It was strange being out of bed so late with no one else around. Those portraits were still watching her. The oil-textured eyes sent a deep chill through her chest. She was now more confident there weren't any hidden cameras around, like she'd previously thought, but she would never trust their eyes.

Lily began reading through the year group noticeboards, starting with the sixth formers.

At the top of the noticeboard was an A4 sheet for the Christmas Carol service. To be held in the abbey, on Saturday the 20th of December. One day after the last official day of term. Parents were invited, but Lily hadn't asked hers if they would come. To walk fourteen miles to watch a school concert is quite an ask in the middle of winter, and not to mention the walk home afterwards.

At the very end of the row of noticeboards, Lily came up to the third-year noticeboard. Flicking through the posters of credit awards and sports announcements she saw her name written in black and white. She was listed on the hockey team. Little, un-sporty, Lily Thicke was down to play in defence, in a home match against Brickstowe School, this coming Wednesday afternoon.

"I can't believe it," Lily whispered to herself.

She laughed out loud. The sound echoed around the food hall. The echo of her own laugh made her hairs stand on end. She froze and listened when the silence returned, wanting to hear if anyone was coming. The hall and corridors beyond were still. She decided she'd better head back to bed for the night. Finding out she'd made the hockey team was enough excitement for the evening, plus she knew too well that lessons were no fun at all after a sleepless night.

Lily left the food hall full of smiles. She honestly couldn't believe how much she was enjoying being at Winkton Abbey. She felt as if she would be forever grateful to her parents for sending her to such a brilliant place. She appreciated Winkton Abbey so much more having come from a school that didn't care about anything at all, to now being at a school that cared about everything from perfect grammar to haircuts, and from table manners to the way you walked and the way you talked. Winkton Abbey was the best start in life Lily could have asked for.

Her mother always told her, *"It is not the school you go to that makes you, it is you who makes you."* Lily knew she'd said that because she didn't want Lily thinking just because she attended a good school it would automatically make her clever. She would still have to work very hard. Lily felt as though she *was* working as hard as she could, and she hoped her parents would be proud of her with the report she would take home at the end of the term.

The end of the corridor loomed. Turning right would take her to bed, and turning left would lead to Miss Warple's office. Something inside her told her to go left towards the office.

She did so without giving any great thought to it.

When she arrived outside of the office, it was as if there was a voice inside of her, goading her to get inside. She tried the door handle. It was locked. Lily took a step back and wondered how a thief like Robert might get inside. *Ah-hah,* she thought, *that's so simple it's stupid.* Above Miss Warple's office were roof tiles in the ceiling which had been built over the top of a partition wall.

Lily hopped up onto the bench outside of Miss Warple's office, and pulled herself up onto the top of a filing cabinet beside the bench.

Pushing a ceiling-tile loose, she stood up, poking her head into the hole.

Lily switched on her torch, lighting up a network of tiles that spread for as far as the light carried.

She couldn't believe her luck. Just a couple of feet over the wall and she would be able to drop down, through the ceiling tiles, into Miss Warple's office, and all without anyone ever knowing.

Lily lifted herself up through the gap, and up above the roof tiles. The spider webs were just about bearable, but the shadows of the spiders sitting in their webs made them look like eight-legged monsters, watching her with a hundred glowing eyes. She told herself they were only tiny, and they couldn't do her any harm. She put the ceiling-tile back in place behind her. Shuffling forward a few tiles she lifted one out where she thought the office might be. She didn't half feel clever when she saw Miss Warple's desk right beneath her.

Lily dropped down onto another filing cabinet, and suddenly wondered why she was risking being caught in the Headmistress' office.

There's a reason why we do everything, she thought, *so what am I doing here?*

Lily's feet touched the floor. She shone the torch around the room. She saw the five-hundred pounds sitting on Miss Warple's desk. She found it odd that there were no photos of family around, but then knowing Miss Warple, perhaps that wasn't so odd.

Lily scanned the room, seeing four large filing cabinets against the back wall and a piece of artwork on the side wall, of a lake and a watermill. Apart from a computer and three chairs, that was all there was inside of Miss Warple's office.

Lily moved the torchlight back to the filing cabinet. *I need to see Robert Groom's file. That's what I'm doing here!* She pulled open the middle drawer of the second cabinet along. She knew it was wrong to be going through other people's files, but this stealing was serious, and if Miss Warple wasn't interested in tackling it, well Lily thought that someone had to.

She fingered through the files. *Herbert, Shawn... Heston, Philip... The letter G must be the next drawer up,* she thought.

Lily opened the top drawer and began flicking through. *Galloway, John… Gosling, Lester… Groom, Robert…*

Lily took out Robert's file and laid it on Miss Warple's desk. She took a moment, hoping she would find something worth taking this risk for. She'd gotten into so much trouble already for trying to help Ameshin. Even so, she knew she would do it all again. There was something about doing the right thing that made Lily feel proud, even when others told her it was wrong.

Lily flicked through paperwork listing Robert's address, previous schooling, emergency numbers, and medical history. On the fifth sheet of the file a Winkton Abbey, school-headed-letter heightened her attention.

She read it through.

Dear Mr Groom,

This is a second reminder letter.

It has come to our attention your cheque for the first term of boarding, made out to "Minkton Abbey School" cannot be banked due to the spelling error in the name.

We ask you kindly to resubmit the cheque by the end of term, no later than the 15th of December. If there are any problems with doing so, please contact our administrations department at your earliest convenience.

Yours sincerely,

E. J. Warple

Miss Elizabeth J. Warple
Headmistress
Winkton Abbey

"Robert hasn't paid his school fees. That's why he shouldn't be here. Exactly as I thought," Lily said to herself.

The door handle moved. Lily spun her head and stood still. Her eyes locked onto the handle. It moved again. Her heart bounced off the walls. Her tongue dried up, horrified at who could be on the other side.

Lily composed herself.

She tidied away the file, putting the folder back in the drawer. She slid the cabinet drawer shut. Someone was still trying to get in.

They don't have a key. Otherwise they'd be in by now. Robert must be here for the five-hundred pounds, Lily thought. *What timing. I'm going to catch him.*

She switched off her torch and hid under the desk. Then she realised there was a gaping hole in the ceiling.

Too late.

The door was open.

Torchlight flooded the room. Lily held her breath. There were no voices, only the flickering of torchlight. Whoever it was, was alone and they didn't know she was there. They hadn't yet seen the tile missing from the ceiling, and even if they did they might not think much of it.

I have to see who it is, Lily told herself. *I'll regret it if I don't.*

She poked her head out from under the desk. The person there was doing something with the picture on the wall. Lily caught a sight of a safe behind the picture. She poked her head out a little more. *It is Robert Groom. I've caught him.*

Torchlight swung around, catching sight of her eyes in the dark. Lily ducked, smacking her head on the desk. Everything went black.

*

Lily heard voices, seeing bright lights. Her head hurt.

"She's waking up. Now we'll see what she has to say for herself," said Miss Warple.

"Calm down, Miss Warple," a man said, who was a policeman, from what Lily could see through her blurred vision.

"My head," said Lily.

Matron Jackie helped Lily sit up. "You've had a nasty knock there, dear," she said.

"Never mind her head. She's fine, look at her. Oh I can't bear to look at her," said Miss Warple, quite distressed by finding an unconscious pupil in her office, who it seemed to her had been up to no good.

"Miss Thicke, are you all right to talk now?" the policeman said.

"Yes, I've got so much to tell you," said Lily.

"Well, we don't want to hear it. I want her out, Sergeant Harper. I cannot forgive a pupil for breaking into my office and stealing, of all things," said Miss Warple.

"Stealing? I wasn't stealing anything," said Lily. She got to her feet a little too quickly, and felt a queasiness floating behind her eyes.

By the look on Miss Warple's face she didn't believe a word of it. "I came into my office, first thing this morning, to find you lying on the floor with my five-hundred pounds in your hands. You obviously lost your balance when you were trying to escape back through the ceiling. Now, which part of being caught with your hand in the honey jar don't you understand?" she said.

"Stealing your five-hundred pounds?" said Lily in shock.

"Yes!" said Miss Warple. "I've never seen such a sore loser. Breaking into my office to steal it from me. I won it fair and square. You'll get what's coming to you, girl!"

The reality of what Robert had done dawned on Lily. He had put the money in her hands, while she was unconscious, and he left her to be caught.

"But that's not what happened," said Lily. "Robert Groom broke in here. He took something. I know he did. I saw him," said Lily.

166

"Nothing is missing from the room, Lily," said Sergeant Harper. "What do *you* think, Miss Warple? I'm good friends with Lily's uncle, and I don't want to be arresting young girls incorrectly."

"Arresting?" said Lily, becoming frantic

Miss Warple gave Lily her famous stare as she answered the sergeant. "She has been sneaking around and causing trouble ever since she arrived. It was only because her desperate parents paid for three years upfront that I even let her into this school. I want this girl's locker searched to see what else she's been up to," she said.

"Come with me, Lily," Sergeant Harper said. He took her by the shoulder and marched Lily down the corridors, in front of everyone that was gathering to see what the police were doing at the school.

This was more embarrassing than the school laughing at the toilet roll in her shoe; this was more embarrassing than being suspended for a week and picked up in a police car; and this was more embarrassing than being the poorest girl in school.

Everyone that looked at Lily assumed she was a thief. Lily's eyes began to tremble. The hallways filled up with everyone trying to get a look. Jinny Green followed along behind her Auntie Warple. *You're a thief. You don't belong at this school.* People were saying.

"That's not true. I wouldn't steal a thing from anyone," said Lily, being moved along by the heavy hands of Sergeant Harper.

"Here we are then, the moment of truth. Open up your locker," said Miss Warple.

Lily fiddled for the key on her necklace. Ameshin and Ben pushed their way to the front of the crowd.

"Lily, we just heard," said Ameshin.

"Hurry up, girl," said Miss Warple.

Lily unlocked her locker. The door swung open.

"NO!—NO!" said Ameshin.

Inside was Ameshin's violin case, Ben's watch, and Jinny's necklace.

"Ameshin, I—I—" Lily couldn't speak.

"Lily Thicke you are hereby expelled from Winkton Abbey school, for stealing, and for gross misconduct, the likes of which this school has never seen in its one-hundred-year history," said Miss Warple. "Sergeant, take her away." She pointed firmly to the way out.

Ben shook his head at Lily. He looked lost without his smile. Ameshin had gone. Lily said nothing. She could say nothing, the evidence against her was enough to make even *her* think she was guilty.

The sergeant led Lily back through the hallways. The children started to boo at the school thief who had stolen from her friends and pretended to help them.

Lily wasn't sure she could ever get out of this. She wished that she had let it go and stayed out of trouble, like she'd been told to do so many times. She loved being a pupil at Winkton Abbey. She was learning so much; she'd made good friends; she'd been selected for the hockey team; and she didn't want to go back to Stakdale.

*

Lily arrived home with her suitcases. Sergeant Harper tipped his cap to Mrs Thicke before he drove away. Lily's mother had no greeting for Lily. There was no hug to welcome her home. Mrs Thicke held open the door and Lily walked inside her house feeling the most alone that she could ever feel.

For days Lily could hardly eat. She cried herself to sleep. It drove her mad knowing that Robert had done this to her. Nothing else entered her mind, except for Ameshin and Ben. She wanted to tell them it wasn't true; to make them see sense.

Lily's mother came and sat beside Lily on her bed. Lily turned away from her mother with her face full of tears.

"There are two and a half weeks of this term left," said Mrs Thicke. "So, after Christmas, and the New Year, you will return to Stakdale. We're lucky they'll still have you."

Mrs Thicke began to sob.

Lily wanted to explain everything, but she feared that everyone would add lying to her long list of bad behaviours.

It seemed there was nothing she could do.

169

Chapter Fourteen
Old Friends

Lily's expulsion was all that Ameshin heard people talking about for the whole of the following week. Some people believed Lily *was* a thief, and others couldn't quite fathom it. Ameshin escaped all of the gossip by practicing in the music room.

She looked at her old violin, and she didn't know which she'd rather have; her violin back in her hands, or her friend back by her side. Her strings whined with a soft sadness. Only Ameshin's eyes showed more unhappiness than her music. She took the bow away from the strings. She couldn't concentrate on playing with so much on her mind.

"Oh, Lily. Stupid, Lily. Your life could have been so different," Ameshin sighed to herself.

"Do you think she did it?" a voice said, which came from a dark corner of the room.

Ameshin jumped, not aware that someone else was in the room. "Mr Stoot?" she said. "How do you move about so silently?"

"Years of being ignored has seemed to help," said Mr Stoot. "You do play well, young Ameshin."

"Thank you—what are you doing back? If you don't mind my asking?" said Ameshin.

"Miss Warple *had* to re-instate me after they found the *'real'* thief," said Mr Stoot.

"You don't think it was Lily?" said Ameshin.

"I've never seen anyone as devoted to helping her friends as Lily was. And I don't expect it would have been the smartest way to do it—hiding everything you stole inside your own locker," said Mr Stoot.

"I don't know what to believe anymore," said Ameshin.

"What does your heart tell you?" said Mr Stoot.

"That Lily was the best friend I've ever had," said Ameshin.

"Don't give up on her. She never gave up on you," said Mr Stoot.

"What could be done? Miss Warple will never believe that anyone other than Lily was the thief," said Ameshin.

"At first Miss Warple didn't believe there was a thief at all. What does it matter what she thinks? You need to listen to what Lily was telling you," said Mr Stoot.

"Robert Groom," said Ameshin. "Lily told us that he was the real thief, but now all of us have got back the necklace, the watch, and the violin; and the five hundred pounds was never taken; and the safe that Lily saw in Miss Warple's office was empty. Miss Warple said that she'd even forgotten the safe was behind that picture, and there was nothing in it."

"You're telling me nothing was taken then? Except for the things that it appears Lily stole?" said Mr Stoot.

"That's right. Nothing was taken," said Ameshin.

"I don't think a thief is a very good thief if he gives everything back, do you?" said Mr Stoot.

"You're right, something doesn't add up," said Ameshin.

"I'd keep an eye on that Robert Groom. He seems a likeable lad at most times, but there's still a behaviour about him that I can't put my finger on," said Mr Stoot.

Ameshin smiled. "You really think it wasn't Lily?" she said.

Mr Stoot smiled back with his two missing teeth, looking a lot friendlier now than when Ameshin had first caught sight of him. "What do I know, eh? I've only seen about a million children come and go at this place," he said. "I must get on. Lots to do." And with that, Mr Stoot left Ameshin alone with her thoughts.

Ameshin placed her violin under her chin. She rested her bow on the strings. *This is no time for practice,* she thought. Ameshin packed away her violin and raced across the school. She ran into the sports hall, where she knew Ben would be playing indoor cricket.

Ben was mid-bowl as she ran in. He smashed the wickets at the other end of the nets, and celebrated as if playing in a test match for England.

"Ben, I need your help," Ameshin called across the hall.

"Hey, Ameshin. What is it?" said Ben.

"Do you think Lily did it? I mean do you think Lily really stole our things?" said Ameshin.

"The more I think about it, the more stupid it sounds. But what are we supposed to do about it? Lily's been expelled. No one has ever been allowed back after they've been expelled," said Ben.

"We need to figure all of this out. We're missing something obvious," said Ameshin.

"If it was obvious I think the police and Miss Warple would have figured it out," said Ben.

"Unfortunately, they haven't. They only saw what they wanted to see. We need to look beyond the details," said Ameshin.

"Let's keep an eye on Robert and see what he's up to then shall we?" said Ben.

The bell rang for the end of lunch, and Ben and Ameshin both had double Physics to get to. It was a comfort to the both of them they had each other to fill the void of missing Lily. They walked on their way to the physics lab from the sports hall. Coming around a corner they found themselves walking behind Robert Groom. Something caught Ameshin's eye almost instantly. On the bottom of Robert's left shoe a white label flashed every time he lifted his heal. Ameshin tapped Ben's arm and pointed it out.

Ben looked up at her. "New shoes," he whispered.

They noticed something else too. Robert was unwrapping a packet of sweets.

"And someone's been to the tuck shop over lunch, with their new-found money," said Ameshin.

Ben and Ameshin knew that if Lily's observations had been correct, and if Robert had had holes in his shoes, and had never had any money to spend at the tuck shop, this was clearly no longer the case.

Ben stopped walking. "I'm not going to lesson," he said.

"Well if you're not, neither am I. Come on, let's go and see Lily. I know how we can get there," said Ameshin.

*

Mr Stoot slid the minibus door shut and jumped into the driver's seat. "You'll get me into a lot of trouble for this—I hope," he said to Ben and Ameshin, rubbing his hands together, laughing at himself, and they were soon well on their way to Lily's house.

Lily opened the front door.

Ameshin jumped at her, wrapping her arms around her without saying a word. Ben dived in with a hug, and the three of them smiled and laughed at being back together.

"How did you know I didn't do it?" said Lily.

Mr Stoot stepped into view.

"We had some help figuring it out," said Ameshin.

"Come in, all of you, come in," said Lily.

They went through to Lily's lounge. Tissues were all over the floor, and Ben and Ameshin realised that Lily had been sitting at home for over a week, crying by herself. They felt awful, and ashamed they hadn't believed in their friend.

"Robert's got new shoes," said Ameshin.

"And he's been raiding the tuck shop," said Ben.

"So all of a sudden he's got money. I wonder if he's paid his school fees somehow as well?" said Lily.

"What do you mean?" said Ameshin.

"I found a letter to his father asking him to hurry up and pay the school fees. There was an obvious spelling mistake on his cheque, which meant it could never be banked. A handy mistake to make if you're trying to stall for time," said Lily.

"What I can't understand is why he gave back all of the things he stole?" said Ben.

"That is unusual for a thief, but clever," said Lily. "I've been thinking a lot about that. He must have stolen something worth a lot more than he'd already stolen, and because I'd seen him in Miss Warple's office, he had to stop my snooping somehow. And he did a really good job of it," said Lily.

"Yes, but what did he steal?" said Ameshin. "There's nothing missing."

"I need to get back into Miss Warple's office. Are you with me?" said Lily.

Ameshin and Ben didn't hesitate to nod in agreement, even though they both knew that they could end up being expelled like Lily.

"The access to Miss Warple's office has been blocked off through the roof," said Mr Stoot. "But I can still get you in."

"Thank you, Mr Stoot. Tomorrow morning, during assembly, that's when we'll do it," said Lily.

Chapter Fifteen

The Bell

Upon returning to school, Ameshin and Ben were given a detention by Mr Fowle for missing their physics lesson. It was Ben's second detention of the term, which he was rather miffed about. Ameshin made the comment it was only her first detention, though Ben was quick to remind her she'd been suspended for a whole week earlier in the term.

Ameshin could never forget that, her father reminded her every time they spoke on the phone. She just hoped nothing more serious would come from helping out Lily. Regardless of whatever happened to her and Ben, she thought they were doing the right thing helping Lily, and she knew they would deal with and accept any further punishment that may be coming.

In the food hall, Ben and Ameshin kept an eye on Robert while they were having their dinner.

He was sitting alone. He hardly ever spoke to anyone. He was a bit of an enigma some of the children would say. There were many different opinions of him that went around the school; some thought he was helpful; some thought he was spoilt; some thought he was grumpy; and some thought he was quite kind. Ben and Ameshin were talking about all of the things they had heard about him.

177

"I don't care whether people love him or hate him, he's the reason that Lily isn't at this school anymore," said Ameshin.

"Do you think he's too smart to be caught?" said Ben.

"Too smart? For all three of us? I don't think so," said Ameshin. "He'll slip up somewhere. Criminals always do."

"Do you think we'll get another detention for missing tomorrow's assembly?" said Ben.

Ameshin nodded while swallowing a mouthful of chocolate pudding. "Maybe a discredit too," she said.

"Oh, great," said Ben. He slid a second helping of chocolate pudding towards him to help with his anxiety.

*

The night before the planned break-in to Miss Warple's office felt longer than any other. Lily couldn't sleep. The next day of her life meant too much. If she didn't solve the crime, then she was going back to Stakdale. Not only that, but her parents, and everyone else would think she was a thief and they would think that way forever.

In her mind, Lily went over and over being inside of Miss Warple's office, trying to think what Robert was doing there. *Maybe he had access to computer passwords and stole some money with some cover up accounting or something,* Lily thought to herself. She just didn't know. What she did know was, the answer would be found inside Miss Warple's office.

After a thousand tosses and turns, and ten times as many thoughts, she managed to get off to sleep, with a few hours of darkness remaining.

*

It was a dull and rainy Thursday morning. The school children hurried across the field to the abbey for morning assembly. Ben and Ameshin waited outside of the main house for Lily and Mr Stoot to arrive.

Mr Stoot came bursting out of the front door of the main house. Ben and Lily's hearts sank. "Sorry, you two, I've overslept," he said. "I'm off to get Lily now. You'd better get over to assembly."

"But assembly will be over by the time you get Lily back. There won't be time to get into Miss Warple's office now," said Ameshin.

"One of you will think of something, I'm sure," said Mr Stoot, running off to the minibus.

Ameshin sighed. "Come on, Ben, assembly it is," she said.

They scooted inside of the abbey, only just in front of Miss Warple. Which was lucky. Anyone coming in behind her had an automatic detention.

Ameshin didn't sing a word of the opening hymn. She couldn't help thinking it was about now they should be looking for clues, not singing, or sitting and listening to whatever was about to pour out of Miss Warple's mouth. The hymn came to an end and the school were commanded to sit.

"I will start with some news," said Miss Warple. "Because of recent events, and you all know which those are, we will be having cameras placed outside of my office and outside the gates of the school."

The children mumbled amongst themselves. *'It won't be long before they have cameras in the showers,'* one of the fifth formers called out.

"Calm down," said Miss Warple. "I know cameras are not a popular choice of security. That is why we have limited them to these two areas. The cameras will be going up this afternoon. If you see some strange men around, they are here for a good reason."

Ameshin leant in to Ben. "How are we going to get past cameras?" she whispered.

"We'll have to get Lily into the office before this afternoon," said Ben.

Ameshin's smile was full of nerves. She knew this had just become a lot riskier than missing one assembly.

"We have one week left before you all go home for Christmas," said Miss Warple. "There are still Christmas concert tickets left for parents. Let's get these sold and have another full service this year, shall we?"

Miss Warple went on to talk about the football, rugby, hockey, and netball teams. She handed out credits for good performances. The hockey match that Lily was supposed to play in finished 4-4, and Izzy got a credit for Tregonwell for scoring a hat-trick. She stood up and took the applause. Ameshin couldn't help but wonder what the score might have been if Lily had been playing in defence. She'd seen how good Lily was now and thought it a shame she'd had her first ever competitive game of hockey taken away by a lie. *All the more reason to get her back to the school,* she thought.

Miss Warple continued, "With one week to go of the term, the Winkton Abbey Cup standings are; Drake remain top with 105 credits. Tregonwell second with 99 credits. Edison in fourth with 80 credits, and Hardy bottom with 75 credits. There is a long way to go until the end of the school year, but it would be a sweet Christmas to be sitting top of the school league, so do your best. School dismissed."

No one was in a hurry to get back out into the rain. The whole school waddled out of the abbey and spread out across the fields heading to their lessons.

Ben and Ameshin walked in silence. Ben wasn't sure if they were supposed to be thinking silently, or whether they were rueing a missed chance to get into Miss Warple's office with Mr Stoot having overslept. Either way, they didn't utter a word on the way to the maths classroom.

The maths teacher, Mr Woodcock, set some sums and equations on the board, and the class were told to sit in silence and complete the tasks. Ameshin knew teachers often did this when they hadn't caught up with marking their homework. It kept the children nice and quiet while the teacher did the work they should have done the night before. The funny thing was, teachers thought no one knew about them doing it, but children aren't that stupid.

Someone knocked at the door. Mr Woodcock looked over and waved them in.

Mr Stoot entered.

"What is it, Stoot?" said Mr Woodcock.

Mr Stoot was looking between Ben and Ameshin and doing a funny flick with his head. "I need two pupils to help me move something for ten minutes," he said.

"If you must, but hurry them back will you? Who will help the caretaker?" said Mr Woodcock, to the class.

A flurry of hands went up, including Ameshin's and Ben's, once they'd realised what was going on.

Mr Woodcock went to choose two pupils, but Mr Stoot quickly trumped him.

"You and you," said Mr Stoot, pointing out Ben and Ameshin. "Thank you, Mr Woodcock. I won't keep them long."

Mr Woodcock grunted. He was already back to ticking his way through the pile of homework on his desk.

Ameshin, Ben, and Mr Stoot hurried along the corridor.

"Did you get Lily?" Ameshin asked Mr Stoot.

"She's here and hiding in the library. No one ever goes in the library these days," said Mr Stoot.

Lily was sitting at a table, hidden behind a tall stack of books.

"It's great to see you in that uniform again," said Ameshin.

"Thanks, Amie. I just hope no one else sees me in it," said Lily.

"We've got to move quickly. Warple is having a camera installed outside her office this afternoon," said Ameshin.

"No one told me that," said Mr Stoot. "I have a spare key, like I do for all of the doors, but no one can be caught on camera using it. I'll get fired again."

"Don't worry, Mr Stoot, we'll be in and out of Miss Warple's office before the cameras are up," said Ameshin.

"I don't see how," Mr Stoot said. "Miss Warple spends all day in her office."

"Here's what we're going to do," said Ameshin. "Lily and I will wait right here. Mr Stoot, you and Ben will go into the main hallway, and when the break-time bell stops ringing you will wait thirty seconds until the hallway is full, at which point you will break the glass of a fire alarm and set off the bell."

"You've been practising your sneakiness," said Lily.

"I've learnt from the best," said Ameshin. "And then, after everyone realises the bell isn't a drill, you will run down the corridors, yelling '*FIRE, FIRE*', until the whole school, except for me and Lily, will be out on the front lawn."

Lily's face brightened up. "Miss Warple's office will be empty for at least a few minutes, and there'll be no one around to recognise me, either," she said.

"Here's the key to the office," said Mr Stoot. "Come on Ben, let's get ready to call for a fire. The break-bell is due any moment."

Lily and Ameshin sat in the library in silence, hoping Miss Warple wouldn't ignore the fire bell or the calls for a fire.

The clock on the wall ticked out loud.

The second hand ticked across the minute hand to read 11am, and the clock kept on ticking aloud. The end-of-lesson bell blasted out for five seconds. The girls watched the second hand keep on ticking.

Tick. Tick. Tick.

It flicked its way around the clock. The bell blasted again. It kept on ringing.

Lily pictured pupils all over the school, looking at each other. First wondering if it was a faulty break-bell, then wondering if it was a fire-bell. She imagined a tingle happening somewhere inside each and every one of them, once they realised the fire-bell is not an exercise.

Ben and Mr Stoot had done their job. From the start of the bell to fifty seconds later, staff and pupils were filing out onto the front lawn, without knowing what was going on. And the same fifty seconds was how long Lily and Ameshin had counted before they ran out of the library.

"How long do you think we have?" said Ameshin.

"The closest fire station is a fifteen-minute drive from here," said Lily. "But I'd bet Miss Warple will come looking for a fire herself within five minutes."

The girls rushed around corners and sprinted up hallways. Lily was too quick for Ameshin, but she ran ahead knowing Ameshin would catch her up. When Ameshin did catch up, Lily had already unlocked Miss Warple's office door.

"Let's give ourselves three minutes in here, to be safe," said Lily. "I'm not having you get caught helping me."

"I'll time it. You do what you've got to do," said Ameshin.

Lily started looking around Miss Warple's office. The computer was on. She wanted to test her theory on Robert accessing the school's banks accounts. Clicking on internet history she scanned websites for any clues. The history had been recently cleared. She searched through the files for Robert Groom, but nothing unexpected flashed up.

"It must have been something inside the safe," said Lily. She pushed the picture frame to the side. "I saw Robert push this picture aside to get to the safe."

"Miss Warple has made it clear the safe was empty. She told the whole story to the school. She even said she'd forgotten about the safe, it hadn't been used in so long," said Ameshin.

Lily took a seat in Miss Warple's chair. She looked around the desk. The five-hundred pounds was no longer there. That made sense.

"One and a half minutes," said Ameshin.

Lily stared into mid-air for inspiration and sighed with all hope fading. She looked at the picture on the wall for the first time. She'd seen it there, to push it out of the way to get to the safe, but this was the first time she'd really looked at it.

Lily got out of the chair and came up close to the picture. "Where have I seen this picture before?" she said.

It was a sketch of a mill and its lake, with a meadow in the background. It was clearly signed in the bottom corner by an artist named *John Constable*.

"Robert Groom," said Lily, "he drew a picture just like this in art. Miss Packham showed me one that she was marking. This is it, this is what he stole. Miss Warple must have had an original John Constable artwork in here and she didn't even know it, but somehow Robert did. He perfected a fake copy and swapped the real one for it, without anyone knowing anything was missing. The picture will be worth tens, or even hundreds of thousands of pounds, if it's an original."

"We've got thirty seconds," said Ameshin.

"How are we going to prove it? The real picture will be long gone by now. Robert will have sold it to a private reseller or even a private collector," said Lily.

Ameshin had a thought, but with no time to explain she grabbed the phone on Miss Warple's desk without saying a word.

"What are you doing? Who are you calling?" said Lily.

Ameshin was too busy pressing buttons on the phone to answer. She started shouting in Japanese over the noise of the fire-bell. She gave the person on the other end no time to speak back. It sounded like she was shouting commands, and not taking no for an answer. The argument was one sided, and Ameshin was winning.

She slammed the phone down. Miss Warple stormed into the office.

Her eyes ballooned, repulsed by the scene. "THICKE!" she shouted. "I thought— I cannot— This is— GET. OUT. OF. THIS. SCHOOL," Miss Warple screamed above the sound of the fire-bell.

She grabbed Lily by the ear, dragging her along, marching her out of the office. "And you," she pointed to Ameshin. "Come with me."

Lily protested, "Ameshin was only telling me not to be so stupid, miss. She's got nothing to do with this."

Miss Warple dragged Lily and Ameshin down a bell-rattling corridor. "Is that true?" she shouted.

"Yes, miss. I didn't want her to get into any more trouble," said Ameshin.

"I will deal with you later. WILL SOMEONE PLEASE TURN OFF THESE BLASTED BELLS!" Miss Warple yelled.

The bells stopped ringing as if they'd heard her. Ameshin's arm was released and she watched Lily be dragged off down the hall and turfed out the front door.

Once again, the whole school crowded together to watch Lily Thicke, the girl who wouldn't learn, be escorted out of the gates of Winkton Abbey.

"If I see you back here one more time, I swear by the Gods of all teachers that I will have you taken away from your parents and locked up in a juvenile detention centre for a very long time. Heed my words, girl, I am more serious than I have ever been," said Miss Warple.

Lily had no words.

She turned, dropped her head, and she began the walk home.

Chapter 16
The Package

"You are grounded for a very long time," said Mrs Thicke when she opened the door to a sorry looking Lily.

The rainy walk home made Lily look like a little lost puppy. Wet hair slapped across her face; wet white shirt hugging tight to her skin; and heavy, sad eyes.

Lily had no words of protest. She'd expected to be punished, but the grounding was going to put a stop to any attempt in clearing her name and having Robert Groom revealed a master thief and scammer.

"Do you not have anything to say, Lily?" said Mr Thicke.

She did not. Her body language said everything. She was tired, angry, hungry, although she didn't feel like eating, and she was frustrated at exactly how she had arrived at this moment. The world was fighting against everything she did, and she didn't know why.

Lily found herself in some kind of daze, still standing on the doorstep, in the rain, as if not allowed in the house because she had been so terrible.

Mrs Thicke waved a hand in front of Lily's face. "Can you at least promise us you will not return to that school. Miss Warple was adamant on the phone that she will follow through on her threat to take you away from us, and I believe she would be very capable of it."

Lily wanted to promise. But how could she when she had uncovered the real secret and solved the mystery that had been going on under everyone's noses all this time. An art theft, of astronomic proportions.

"I won't go back to that school," said Lily, after some thought. "No one will believe what I found out anyway."

She walked in between Mr and Mrs Thicke and went straight to the bathroom.

A long soak in the bath helped her clear her head somewhat. She told herself over and over again that she had done nothing wrong and had nothing to feel bad about. It made her sad to think that Ben, Ameshin, and Mr Stoot, were the only people in the world who thought the same way she did. She wanted to tell her mind to start thinking that no one else's opinion mattered and say to hell with everyone who thought she was no good, but she didn't think she could ever do that.

When Lily was in trouble, or sometimes even just when it was raining, as it still was, she liked to go and sit in the shed at the bottom of the garden. The shed was the closest thing the Thicke family had to a summer house, but it was only an old, wooden shed with two small windows and a stable door. It was cold and damp, yet Lily did her best to keep it clean and tidy. She'd put up a map of Dorset on the wall and marked out some of her favourite places. She was staring at the map. Staring at the dot that was Winkton Abbey School. Alone, wrapped in a blanket, sitting in an old armchair she'd rescued from a skip long ago, she sat and poured out her thoughts.

Drops of water dribbled down the windows. The sound of rain falling on the roof helped to clear her mind.

I wonder who Ameshin was on the phone with? I don't suppose it matters now, but I hope she isn't in any more trouble over this mess, she thought.

It was time, Lily decided, that she would give up on trying to prove she wasn't the thief, and time to give up on trying to prove that Robert was. After all, she was the only one who had come out of this badly.

There's no real harm done. She thought. *I'll just go back to how things were before Winkton Abbey. Everyone has their valuables back, and if Robert has managed to pull off the theft of a famous artwork, good luck to him, I suppose. He's outsmarted us all. And my parents are going to get most of their money back anyway.*

It didn't seem to matter what she told herself, she still felt awful for having to leave a school that she'd grown to love. One thing Lily knew she would regret was not seeing Ameshin play a solo at the Christmas concert, just over a week away.

She wondered if she could somehow sneak into the abbey and watch, hidden away somewhere, but her mother really had made her promise she wouldn't go back.

It was getting dark outside, Lily thought she'd better go in, before her parents began to think she'd run away somewhere. She still didn't feel like talking to them and telling them the whole truth of everything. For now, no one was speaking at all in the Thicke household.

Lily ran inside and went straight to bed.

*

Monday at Winkton Abbey arrived. It was the beginning of the last week of the autumn term. Everyone in the school was starting to relax, and Christmas carols were playing in the food hall, where a tree and colourful decorations brightened up the lunch hall's wood-panelled walls.

Ameshin wasn't so relaxed, or excited about Christmas. She would be heading back to Japan this coming Saturday, a few hours after the end of the concert. She wasn't feeling at all festive with everything that had gone on. She kept herself to herself. Even Ben couldn't get a word out of her. Ameshin had shared her knowledge of the stolen artwork with no one, not even Ben, nor Mr Stoot. She didn't want to give anything away to the wrong person, not knowing who else might be involved, who else might overhear.

The school-gossips, like Trinny Brent and Bethany Cahill, and Izzy's sister, Emily, asked what she knew, but Ameshin refused to speak to anyone about what had happened in Miss Warple's office during the fire alarm. She knew that if Robert heard Lily had figured it all out, he would disappear, and that would ruin Ameshin's plan.

Ever since Lily had been banished last Friday, Ameshin had been doing something rather strange at 11pm every night.

For the fourth night in a row, at 11pm, Ameshin sneaked out of the main house, into the woods, and out of the school grounds through the hole in the fence. Half a mile down the hill she saw the familiar sight of the red-brick bridge which towered over the road leading up to the school.

She waited there for an hour.

Nothing happened.

After the fourth non-event, she went back into the school and returned to bed.

The next three nights, Ameshin followed the same pattern at 11pm, waiting by the bridge, for an hour each time.

Still nothing happened.

The more that time went on, the more she worried her plan was not going to work. The last night of term was quickly upon her, and when everyone else was excited to have broken up for the holidays and in full festive swing for the coming Christmas, Ameshin had other things on her mind.

She sneaked out at 11pm to stand at the bridge for the last time, before she would be returning to Japan the day after. Tonight, she waited for more than an hour, shivering herself silly out in the frost.

Still nothing happened.

Ameshin closed her eyes, the movement of her eyelids pushed a single tear out the corner of her eye. Sitting under the bridge in the dark. She knew she had lost Lily as a friend forever. She wanted to save her. She wanted to give her back the chance of the life her parents had worked and saved so hard to give her.

She got up to walk back to school.

A noise somewhere in the distance made her halt. She daren't move. She opened her ears.

She heard someone walking close by. No, it wasn't footsteps, it was a car, driving slowly over gravel on the road. She slid out of view, into dense bushes. From the other side of the bridge headlights lit up the road.

The car stopped.

Ameshin poked her head out of the bush, *this must be it,* she thought. Someone got out of the car and shut the door. Ameshin came out of hiding to see a man dressed in sleek black, holding a package in leather gloved hands. He shouted something in Japanese. Ameshin hurried over, shouting back as she ran. The package was offered. Ameshin took it.

"Thank you," she said, bowing her head in respect.

The man got into the car, reversing off, without saying another word.

Ameshin closed her eyes in relief, tasting the salt of another tear. The sweetest salt she had tasted. She blew out a heavy breath and smiled.

"Just in time," she said to herself, hugging the package tight.

*

Some parents were already beginning to arrive an hour early. The Christmas Carol Service was starting at 11:30am.

Ameshin looked positively gleeful as she entered the food hall swinging her violin case back and forth with every happy stride.

Ben spotted her. He couldn't believe she was smiling.

"That's more like it," he said. "Are you looking forward to going home, or is it playing in the concert you're excited about?"

"It's something much more exciting than that," said Ameshin. "Lily's coming back to school today,"

"Lily's coming back? Today?" said Ben.

"Be quiet," said Ameshin, calming him down. "No one knows yet, and we need to keep it that way."

"Oh, right—I have no idea what you're going on about, but I hardly ever do with you two. I just enjoy the ride," said Ben.

Ameshin chuckled and bounced on her way.

"Where are you going now?" said Ben.

"To sort something out. And have a quick practice," said Ameshin.

"Haven't you practiced enough?" said Ben.

"How can you ever practice enough?" said Ameshin, disappearing out of the dining room door.

Once outside, Ameshin scanned the fields for one thing, a brown tweed blazer. It baffled her that boys didn't wear their jackets when the ground was thick with frost. On this occasion she was glad of it. Tom was much easier to spot. This time he wasn't with his girlfriend, and he wasn't with Jinny, or with his friends either. Tom was taking a walk around the school grounds with his parents.

As Ameshin came closer to Tom and his parents, she hoped he still didn't want that photograph getting out. "Hi Tom, can I borrow you for a moment?" she said.

Tom gave her a blank stare. He must have wondered how he'd let himself get caught kissing a girl by a couple of very pesky third years.

"I wanted to ask you something, about my violin solo today," said Ameshin, giving him an excuse to step away from his parents.

"Of course, happy to help," said Tom.

He walked out of ear shot from his parents. *'Good boy.'* *'Very helpful of you.'* They both said as he walked away.

"Ameshin, now is not a good time for any more bright ideas. You need to give it up," said Tom.

"Listen to me, will you?" said Ameshin.

"Okay, you've got one minute," he said.

Ameshin reeled it all off in thirty seconds. Tom listened carefully about Robert's art skills and the valuable item that had really been stolen, and how Ameshin would prove it. Tom was smart, and as head boy of the school, he couldn't ignore what he'd just been told. He made an excuse to his parents and went inside the main house to make a phone call from the common room. Tom spoke to no one else, only the man on the other end of the line. Ameshin was there listening to the call, and she was entirely satisfied that things were now firmly in place.

"You've done the right thing, Tom, thank you," said Ameshin. "They would never have listened to me or Lily."

"Can you get rid of that photo now please? It was a silly thing really. We got carried away. It was exciting for a while, but then I realised that Hannah's feelings would really be hurt if she found out," said Tom.

"Consider the photo never existed," said Ameshin.

"Thanks, Ameshin. Good luck in the concert," said Tom.

"I need better luck with something else today," said Ameshin.

"Yes, I suppose you do," said Tom.

*

Parents and pupils took their seats in the abbey. The organ played a slowed-down version of *Silent Night* as everyone settled into the church pews and took their seats on the balconies.

Ameshin was up at the front, with the rest of the school orchestra and the choir. She kept her eyes on Robert, who was sitting next to his father. She wondered who he really was, and whether his real name was even Robert Groom.

197

Ameshin knew he was only at this school for one reason, and that was to steal from it.

Every seat in the abbey was soon filled. Some late-comers seemed disappointed having to stand wherever they could, since there was supposed to be a seat for everyone.

The members of the school board had plenty of room up on the balconies, and Ameshin, although feeling a little nervous with what was to come, was glad that everyone involved with the school was here as a witness.

Miss Warple entered, taking her place at the lectern. The congregation stood to welcome her.

"Everybody please sit," said Miss Warple, being a lot more polite now the parents were around. "Welcome to the Winkton Abbey School Christmas Carol Service. Some of you have come from far away, and I hope you are not disappointed with what we have prepared for today's programme. The orchestra and choir have worked extremely hard this term to give you a joyous day, and send you on your way to enjoy a wonderful Christmas with your loved ones. Before we begin, I would like to say a prayer."

The congregation shuffled and bowed their heads.

Miss Warple closed her eyes, and began, "Christmas is a special time for us all to think about how we can make the world a better place. A time we come together and celebrate our love and friendship. A time to forgive those who have wronged—"

The abbey doors banged open.

Everybody opened their eyes, looking up towards the door.

Lily stood there in full school uniform, beaming.

"Hello, Miss Warple, do you forgive me?" she said.

The smile on her face was so big it drove Miss Warple wild with rage.

"LILY THICKE! I have warned you!" Miss Warple screeched.

Lily ran.

Miss Warple was after her like a dog after a hare.

The entirety of the school piled out of the abbey to watch the chase.

Ben caught sight of Ameshin laughing without holding it back. "You two are crazy," he said.

"Come on, we can't miss this," said Ameshin.

She grabbed Ben by the hand, trying to overtake the scrambling congregation. They gained a few metres, but it didn't matter much, the abbey emptied in under thirty seconds.

Lily was much quicker than Miss Warple. She dared to let Miss Warple get close and then put just the right distance between them to make Miss Warple's swiping look ridiculous. Lily ran around in circles on the front lawn, just to make Miss Warple look a little sillier. After a small show of superior agility, Lily bolted in through the door of the main house with Miss Warple flailing behind. The parents and pupils stampeded after them, entering through various entrances to try and get ahead of the game. Lily made sure Miss Warple was right behind her all the way to where she was leading her.

Miss Warple screamed and shouted. Although quite out of breath, she remained determined to catch her prey. Lily came running around a corner where she suddenly stopped, right beside the school lockers.

When Miss Warple turned the corner, she unexpectedly saw Mrs Thicke and a woman, who she'd never seen before. They were stood beside two policemen, one of whom she knew as Sergeant Harper, and the other, whom she didn't know, was Lily's uncle.

"What is going on?" said Miss Warple. "Sergeant Harper, arrest this girl. You have my permission to…"

She stopped talking, aware that parents and pupils continued to fill the corridor from both ends. Hundreds of heads bobbed left and right to get a good view. Some were standing on tip toes and even tables and cabinets in the corridor to see what was going on.

"Excuse me please. Excuse us, coming through," a voice said, moving through the crowd. It was Tom, and he was pushing forward a boy as he moved people out of the way.

The last of the crowd parted and it was Robert who was at the hands of Tom. Lily tensed up, upon seeing Robert Groom in front of her. He made her feel sick she disliked him so much.

Robert's father wasn't far behind his son. "I say, what's all this. Very unnecessary," said Mr Groom. His Queen's-English accent was impeccable.

"That's close enough, Mr Groom," said Sergeant Harper, stepping forward.

"You'd better have a good explanation for all of this," said Mr Groom.

"Well, let's hope so, sir," said Sergeant Harper. "Lily, it's over to you. Everyone let her speak please, no interruptions."

Lily moved into the middle of the only free space in the hallway to address the crowd. Ameshin and Ben pushed their way to the front, sending Lily a thumbs up and a couple of grins.

Lily composed herself with one breath and began to explain everything.

"Earlier in the term, a friend of mine, Ameshin, had her violin stolen. Miss Warple denied that stealing would ever take place at this school, but we knew someone had broken into her locker and taken it. We were suspended for trying to find out who stole it, and after further thefts, Mr Stoot, our caretaker, lost his job. He was accused by Miss Warple of being the thief. We knew that wasn't true. Mr Stoot had worked at this school for decades without ever having stolen a thing, why start now? It didn't make any sense."

Lily was amazed Miss Warple wasn't intervening. Her only protest was a sneer and a stare.

Lily carried on, "Ameshin and I were watching everyone, looking out for suspicious activity. There was none. The thief was clever. It wasn't until I started to notice that Robert never went to the tuck shop to buy sweets, and that he had holes in his shoes, and that he wore a second-hand blazer, just like me, on all accounts, that I realised, Robert Groom was trying to pretend to be someone he was not. He told me he had a rich father who worked in stocks and shares, yet he didn't own a pair of wellies for winter. The facts started to make sense, and we knew that Robert was most likely the thief. A thief who was good at staying silent. He thought no one would ever know what he was up to," said Lily.

"But he didn't steal anything. Everything that was missing was found in *your* locker," said Miss Warple, unable to be silent any longer. Her sneer turned into a smirk.

"I will come to that shortly," said Lily. "I saw the school conker competition as a way to lure the thief into stealing five-hundred pounds. I fully intended to win the competition myself, but Miss Warple came out as the winner. Once she had announced she would keep the money on her desk as a reminder to us all that we might one day be as good as her, I thought that was all that was needed to draw the thief in. For days and nights we watched Miss Warple's office. Nothing happened, and at that point we still hadn't figured out who the thief was. When we did, we decided to watch Robert rather than the office. We had eyes on him at all times. But one night, the eyes in his dorm didn't see Robert sneak out. On the same night, I couldn't sleep. I walked around the school for a while, and something drew me to Miss Warple's office. I figured out a way in through the ceiling tiles, which was surprisingly easy. Once inside I checked the file on Robert Groom. His father had been sent several letters, chasing for the first term's cheque to be paid. The spelling error on the rejected cheque was too obvious to have been a genuine mistake. *Minkton Abbey School*, a five-year-old could have come up with better. When I was inside the office, someone tried the door handle. I put the file away and hid under the desk. There was clicking and scraping at the door, which I presume, was the lock being picked. Someone came into the room. I had a feeling I knew who it was. I looked out from under the desk, but to my surprise I didn't see the person in the room taking the five-hundred pounds from the desk. I saw them pushing a picture on the wall to the side, to reveal a safe behind it."

"That safe was empty. You will not get yourself out of this, no matter what you say," said Miss Warple.

"Miss Warple, give Lily a chance. We all want to see where this is going," Sergeant Harper said.

"You see, Miss Warple, Robert wasn't after the money, or anything to do with the safe. When I went back into your office during the fire alarm, I figured it out. Robert is a brilliant artist. Miss Packham showed me one of his sketches of a watermill. And that sketch was exactly the same as the John Constable drawing that was sitting on your wall in front of that safe. You see, Robert somehow knew the picture in your office was an original Constable. He spent all term perfecting the sketch, and once he had done so, he broke into your office and swapped the pictures over. I didn't see him pushing the picture to the side to get to the safe, I saw him putting *his* picture back in place," said Lily.

Robert wriggled free from Tom's hold. "I've listened to enough of this. What proof do you have? I like to draw. It's just a coincidence," he said.

Lily smiled at him. "I bet Robert couldn't believe his luck when I knocked myself out on the desk. He placed the five-hundred pounds in my hand, broke into my locker and put the other stolen goods inside, turning my friends against me and getting me expelled, so that no one would ever know the truth, or believe me," she said.

"No one does believe you. You're making it all up!" said Robert.

Robert's father stepped forward. "Miss Warple, stop this madness, will you. You know I paid that cheque, albeit a little late, and Robert has fine shoes, there's no holes in them. Look at him," he said.

Sergeant Harper cleared his throat. "Lily, is there any more? We don't have any proof of any of this," he said.

Robert smiled at her.

"Open up his locker," said Lily.

"There's nothing in it. I cleared it out last night to go home for Christmas," said Robert.

"Open your locker, Robert," said Sergeant Harper.

Robert was still smiling. "This is ridiculous," he said, putting his key into his locker. "It's empty, I tell you."

The locker door swung open.

Inside was an object wrapped in white cloth.

"Miss Barnes, over to you," Sergeant Harper said.

Miss Barnes, the woman who no-one knew, stepped forward and took the object out of the locker. She pulled off the sheet, which sent the hallway bursting into chatter. It was a sketch of a watermill, just like Lily had described, and just like the one in Miss Warple's office.

"How?—But I got rid—" said Robert, quickly stopping himself from talking any further.

Miss Barnes studied the sketch with a monocle, turning it over and checking every inch of the paper. The crowd watched on, holding their breath for a verdict.

"An original John Constable, from circa 1850. Sergeant Harper, the boy has committed fraud in my opinion," Miss Barnes said.

Cheering rang through the corridor. Sergeant Harper handcuffed Robert. Lily's mother grabbed and squeezed Lily, with Ben and Ameshin jumping in to congratulate them both. Miss Warple stood as still as death with her mouth wide open.

"I only did what he told me to do!" Robert shouted, pointing at his father.

Robert's father tried to make a run for it. Lily's uncle tackled him to the ground.

"Not so fast, Mr Logan," Uncle Peter said.

"How did you know my name?" he said.

"We didn't. But that was who Ameshin's father bought the picture from, for £150,000.00," said Uncle Peter.

Miss Warple fainted.

Lily looked at Ameshin in disbelief.

Ameshin shrugged her shoulders. "I just told my father to pay whatever it cost. He didn't like it, but I'd already gotten my violin back, which is worth much more than that picture anyway. So really it didn't matter what happened in the end. Hasn't it turned out well?" she said.

Lily, Ben, and Ameshin could do nothing else but roar with laughter and jump about in a huddle. Robert and Mr Logan looked crestfallen upon hearing that the violin was worth more than the John Constable sketch, all along.

A large man in a smart suit stepped out of the crowd. "Ladies and gentlemen, I can assure you a full investigation will be conducted into this matter. Will everyone please head back to the abbey for the rest of the Christmas service," he said.

Miss Warple sat up from her slump, helped by Jinny, to see Mr Groves, the head of the school board addressing the parents.

Mr Groves leant down to her on his way past. "A full report by Monday, Miss Warple—and it had better be good," he said.

Chapter Seventeen

A Fond Farewell

"I've never heard *anything* as beautiful as that," Lily said to Ameshin, following her impeccable and vibrant violin solo. "You put everything you had into it."

The loud applauds and whistles made Ameshin blush as she took her seat beside Lily.

"What's the point in doing something if you don't give it your best?" she said.

"I'll try and remember that one," said Lily.

There was no sign of Miss Warple returning to the abbey. She was, in fact, feeling very lightheaded with everything that had happened, and had decided to hide, resting in the matron's office.

Mr Groves, of the school board, took Miss Warple's place behind the lectern. "Thank you, Ameshin, a remarkable performance," he said, clapping his hands along with everyone else. "That just about concludes our service for today, I would simply like to say a few words, and hand out some further rewards."

Everyone shuffled in their seats quietening down, wondering what Mr Groves had to say.

He cleared his throat. He was rather unused to public speaking. "I have, in front of me, the Winkton Abbey Cup results for this autumn term," he said. "I have seen many gifted children at this school. Some gifted in sports; some gifted in maths; some gifted in courage."

His eyes smiled at Lily for a moment before he continued.

"Intelligence comes in many different forms, you must all remember that. Some people think with their minds, while other people think with their hands or their feet. We all have our own ways of showing our own intelligence, and yours may not always be recognised until much later on in your life. School is a hard place to be sometimes. It is our job at Winkton Abbey to help you find whatever works for you, and we need you to tell us how we can better serve as teachers and as life coaches. We don't have all of the answers, and we won't pretend to, but I want every pupil that comes through the gates of this school to feel comfortable being themselves. To grow as themselves and leave as themselves, having developed a greater understanding of who you are, and hopefully having a better idea of who you want to be. Honesty, boys and girls, is the key to everything. If you dare to be yourself, if you dare to listen to the voice inside of you, I believe you *can* be whatever you want to be."

Everybody stood, and everybody clapped. Mr Groves looked embarrassed, if not proud to stand up there and speak for the school.

The lesson of the first term had all become clear to Lily, Winkton Abbey was the best school she could go to. She would never doubt that again.

The congregation settled back down onto their wooden seats. Mr Groves grew in stature after the unexpected applause.

"What I was just saying is very much a reflection of how well you all do with contributing to the Winkton Abbey Cup," said Mr Groves. "At the end of this term the standings are; Drake House on 109 credits. Tregonwell House 103 credits. Edison House 81 credits. Hardy House 79 credits."

The applause for each house rose up and died down.

"And now on to some extra rewards," Mr Groves said. "Stand up please, Lily Thicke, Ameshin Chi and Benjamin Sawkins."

The three of them stood up. They raised their eyebrows at each other in surprise at their names being called.

Mr Groves held out his hand. "These pupils have shown us all that if you never give up, even when you're being knocked down by everyone around you, that you can still succeed. *Non deficere, et Vincere*. Our school motto; never give up, and you win. These three have lived by these words all term. Their friendship, and attitude, and confidence in themselves is what we want from every Winktonian. So, for what they have achieved this term, I would like to give three credits to each of them. These rewards put Drake and Tregonwell in joint first, and Ben's credits lift Hardy from last place," he said.

The boys and girls from all of the houses cheered and whistled. Ameshin, Lily, and Ben beamed with smiles.

These were the first full credits any of them had been given all term.

Mr Groves calmed the congregation down. "That is not all. Earlier in the year a discredit was given to Lily for not showing up to Miss Warple's office. I do believe Lily was helping Ameshin to look for her missing violin at the time. This discredit is wiped from the record, and that puts Tregonwell House top over Christmas," he said.

Izzy stood up. "Three cheers for Lily," she shouted.

It wasn't just the Tregonwell's who cheered. The whole school cheered for Lily.

"Hoorah. Hoorah. Hoorah."

A man came up to Mr Groves and handed him a piece of paper. Mr Groves hushed the school once more. He raised a pair of spectacles-on-string to the end of his nose and read through the note.

"The police have moved quickly on this," said Mr Groves. "Mr Logan, and Robert Groom, whose real name is Carl Roberts, the adopted son of Mr Logan, have both been charged for conspiring to commit art fraud. Robert has sent a message to the school apologising to you all. His adopted father told him not to make any friends whilst he was here, although he apparently liked many of you. Perhaps the boy will have a better chance of it, now that he is away from Mr Logan. There is good news that Ameshin's father's money, used to buy the stolen artwork, has been recovered, and the sketch has been given a value of £182,000. In light of all of this, Lily, the school board would like to award you a lifetime scholarship award, and free education for as long as you wish to stay with us. That is if you do wish to stay with us?"

Lily stood; mouth wide open. Once again everyone in the school was staring at her. This time she was a hero. This time she was not in trouble.

"Yes, sir! Thank you, sir!" Lily shouted.

Laughs were accompanied by a standing ovation from everyone in the abbey.

Mrs Thicke and Lily stood at the front of the abbey, squeezing each other in a tight embrace.

A tear dropped from the end of Mrs Thicke's nose, landing on Lily's glasses.

Mrs Thicke wiped the droplet from the lens. "You are the best daughter any mother could have," she said. "I have never been as proud of anyone as I am of you today."

Embracing her mother harder, Lily's heart spun with emotion. Ameshin, Ben, and Izzy piled in for a hug.

Lily couldn't believe it. People were clapping for her; her mother was happy; her name was clear; her friends were amazing; and her life at Winkton Abbey School had only just begun.

44566892R00125

Printed in Poland
by Amazon Fulfillment
Poland Sp. z o.o., Wrocław